Michael

AIKIDO TOHO IAI

MEYER
& MEYER
SPORT

Original title: Aikido Toho Iai – Aikido und Schwertkunst
© 2006 by Meyer & Meyer Verlag
Translated by Dr. Michael Russ and Thomas Martin

British Library Cataloguing in Publication Data
A catalogue record for this book is available from the British Library

Michael Russ
AIKIDO TOHO IAI
Oxford: Meyer & Meyer Sport (UK) Ltd., 2006
ISBN-10: 1-84126-183-1
ISBN-13: 978-1-84126-183-6

© 2006 by Meyer & Meyer Sport (UK) Ltd.
Aachen, Adelaide, Auckland, Budapest, Graz, Johannesburg, New York,
Olten (CH), Oxford, Singapore, Toronto
Member of the World
Sports Publishers' Association (WSPA)
www.w-s-p-a.org

Printed and bound in Germany by: B.O.S.S Druck und Medien GmbH, Germany
ISBN-10: 1-84126-183-1
ISBN-13: 978-1-84126-183-6
E-Mail: verlag@m-m-sports.com

Contents

Preface

There are numerous styles and an abundant number of techniques in the world of martial arts. How can you know and be sure which one works and is useful in a life or death situation? What kind of martial art should be learned to ensure effectivity?

Miyamoto Musashi (1584-1645), the most famous swordsman of all time, wrote in his book "The Five Rings" – the Go Rin No Sho in Japanese – that the most important skill in martial arts was how to swing the sword, the Katana. He claimed that the principles of swordfighting were the basis of all other martial arts – which is a thought worth pondering over.

Today people have forgotten that Aikido, founded by MORIHEI UESHIBA, was originally developed from sword combat. Since those times, Aikido has changed more and more into something like a dance and has lost its background of Budo. This is one of the reasons why most other schools do not take Aikido seriously and why it is claimed not suitable for street fighting. The aim of this book is to help rehabilitate the reputation of Aikido as a true martial art, which it undoubtedly is, and put it back in its proper position where it really belongs in the long league of martial arts. For this reason it is necessary to gain an insight into the relationship between the techniques of Aikido and the original sword techniques. In many years of war throughout the different centuries in Japan, the Samurai honed the sword art to the highest perfection possible because the proper use of the sword determined the outcome of a life and death situation. Only the winning party was still alive on a battlefield then.

Aikido Toho Iai is the link between the sword art and the *empty hand* combat techniques. It helps the Aikidoka see the hidden roots of Aikido, so he or she is able to understand the basics of martial arts and improve his or her feeling of motion and body movement. It will also help strengthen your mind, which is one of the most important things to have in a real fight. It can be claimed that martial arts training without practicing with a sword is only a special kind of gymnastics. In a nutshell, the sword is your best teacher.

I owe a great debt of gratitude to my teachers NISHIO Sensei and Paul Müller for all they have given me. I also want to thank my longtime friend Sigurd Mühlherr for his work as Uke and Thomas Martin for his photographic work and support. Further I want to thank my wife Johanna for her patience with me over the years of training, and my son Kevin for the support on the computer. Without them this book would not have been possible.

Michael Russ, M.D., October 2005

PART I
BACKGROUND

1 History of swordsmanship in ancient Japan

Hayashizaki Ryu: Japanese sword art dates back to its beginnings in the Heian period about 800 AD. The sword was used on the battlefield and it had a design different from the later sword of the Samurai, the Katana. Those swords were longer, slimmer and had more curvature. They were worn with the cutting edge facing downward on the left hip, together with armor. These swords were called Tachi or long swords. The techniques used in full armor with these long swords were called Kumi Uchi.

The origin of Iaijutsu, the art of drawing the sword and killing the opponent immediately, was founded by Hayashizaki Jinsuke Minamoto no Shigenobu, born in 1549. His school is called the Hayashizaki Ryu.

Muso Jikiden Eishin Ryu: His successor in the seventh generation, Hasegawa Eishin, adapted the techniques of the Hayashizaki school to the demands of the new swords. These swords were shorter and not so curved as the Tachi before. They were called Katana or Daito and were worn with the cutting edge facing up on the left hip. This style, founded by Hasegawa Eishin, is called Muso Jikiden Eishin Ryu Iaijutsu.

Tenshin Shoden Katori Shinto Ryu: Tenshin Shoden Katori Shinto Ryu, claimed to be the oldest Japanese sword school, is still taught today in its original form. The school was founded by Izasa Choisai Ienao, born in 1447. According to a legend, the techniques were given to the founder by a deity while he was praying under a tree.

Suio Ryu: Suio Ryu, the style of the seagull, was developed about 1615 by Mima Yoichizaemon Kagenobu. Again, it is said, that he was inspired while watching the flight of a seagull. This style is very rare in Japan and Western countries and is claimed to be very remarkable by specialists.

All of these methods were created for drawing a sword and killing the enemy instantly. Therefore all of them are summarized as Iaijutsu schools. After the Meiji restoration in 1868, the wearing of swords in public was forbidden and Iaijutsu techniques lost all their original value. But because they were a treasured part of the Japanese culture, people tried to preserve them.

Iaido: In order to preserve these seemingly useless techniques of Iaijutsu, they were transformed into the art of Iaido. In this style the techniques are no longer used for killing but for improving the mental and spiritual behavior of a Budoka. Its goal is to reach the mental, not the physical ability of the Samurai. Therefore it is no longer important if the techniques work in combat or not, and this is an advantage. It is not necessary as in other martial arts to demonstrate their effectiveness in a real fight. In our times, a fight with swords will not take place any more. Without ever having to prove it, the student can concentrate on the Budo, the constant fight within himself.

Aikido Toho Iai: Aikido Toho Iai was developed by NISHIO Sensei as a result of his extensive experience in Aikido and the different styles of Iaido and Iaijutsu. The connection between the figures carried out with a real sword and the *empty hand* techniques of Aikido is completely new. The meaning of practicing sword techniques is no longer considered to improve only your mental ability when it comes to learning traditional sword forms. It becomes clear that it will also improve your skills in *empty hand* combat. It helps people understand the origin of the technique and to learn which technique is practiced correctly and which is not. The sword becomes the teacher and always teaches the correct technique. If a technique works with the sword, it will work in a real fight as well. If it does not work with the sword the technique may be wrong.

There is a sword form (Kata in Japanese) for every existing Aikido technique. Partner exercises using a wooden sword or stick have also been developed. In this book, 15 forms are described together with an explanation of the Aikido technique. Because the principle is always the same, you can create many other forms of your own.

SHOJI NISHIO Sensei: NISHIO Sensei was born on December 5, 1927 in Gun Ohata Cho, in Shimokia, a prefecture of Aomori, Japan.

In 1942 he started training in Judo in the Takinogawa area, in the north of Tokyo, known today as Kita Ku. In 1950 he began studying Karate and in 1952 he had his first contact with Aikido. Nishio Sensei became a personal disciple of the founder MORIHEI UESHIBA and stayed with him in his Dojo for over 10 years. In 1976 he was awarded the 8th degree black belt in Aikido from Hombu Dojo in Tokyo, Japan.

Apart from that, he is the holder of the 8th degree black belt in Iaido, the 7th degree black belt in Karate and 6th degree black belt in Judo. NISHIO Sensei died on March 15, 2005 at the age of 77 years. In our memory he will live forever.

2 The Japanese sword

There is no other weapon that is as fascinating and mystifying as the sword of the Samurai, the Katana. Many legends exist about it. It is claimed they were made when the moon was shining and that they were so sharp that they could even cut the barrel of a gun. In ancient Japan, these swords were tested on condemned prisoners or dead bodies. The result of the test and the signature of the smith was engraved on the tang and gave the sword a great value. The sword was claimed to be the soul of the Samurai. It was strictly forbidden to touch the blade with the bare hands, and if somebody did that, he was killed instantly by the owner.

Up to now the Japanese sword has lost nothing of its attractiveness. In Japan a smith is allowed to produce only two long swords a month. Once a year the swords of all the smiths are judged and ranked by a commission. Highly ranked swords are very expensive. Over the centuries the smiths developed different methods of sword fabrication. Swords can be classified by age, the area they were made in and by the method used for production. In different areas of ancient Japan like Bizen, Soshu, Yamashiro and Yamato, the smiths produced characteristic swords by using special kinds of steel and also by creating various new forms of blades. Today, the swords from Bizen are believed to be the most typical of the Samurai swords. They have a large blade with a wide point. Swords from Soshu have a slim blade and a small point.

There are two main methods for producing a sword. Both of them use iron sand as the resource of steel and melt it in a special furnace, called Tatara. While melting, the iron is mixed with different quantities of carbon and Tamahagane is produced. The quantity added is responsible for the quality of the steel. A low amount of carbon produces an elastic kind of steel, which does not break easily. A high amount of carbon produces a hard steel, which can be sharpened for cutting, but breaks easily. The ingenious idea these swordsmiths of yore had already was to produce a sword with these two components. Still today, iron pieces, which contain various amounts of carbon, are mixed, folded, heated and hammered into a massive block. This block is reheated and hammered repeatedly and gradually drawn into a U-shaped bar, twice its original length. After making a deep cleft in it, the bar is folded back upon itself and restored to its original length. This process is repeated about 16 times and after that, the steel consists of some 65,000 layers, or even more.

This method is used to produce two different kinds of steel. The first one called Kawagane is very hard and is used for the jacket of the blade. The second one called Shingane is softer and is used for the core. The simple method of creating a sword is to bend the jacket steel into a U shape and place the core steel into the base of the U, forming a sandwich. A more complex method is to use four separate pieces of steel with different amounts of carbon for the two sides, the core and the edge. After heating it in the forge, the block is hammered, reheated and hammered yet again numerous times into the shape of a blade. The sword is flexible and will not break during the fight, but the cutting edge is very hard and can be honed to extreme sharpness.

After that the steel must be hardened by heating and cooling it rapidly. While the edge should be hard for sharpening, the blade should be elastic to absorb the shock of a blow at the same time. Therefore the blade is covered with an isolating coating, made of several agents like clay, pulverized sandstone and some other secret substances the swordsmiths won't reveal. This coating is very thin on the edge and very thick on the blade. When cooling in water, the edge will cool more rapidly than the rest of the blade and will become much harder. A shiny line called the Hammon appears between the hard and the soft metal. This line is very characteristic of the Katana. To prevent chips, there are narrow channels of softer steel, called Ashi, embedded in the hard edge, made by a series of very thin strips of clay perpendicular or at angles to the edge of the sword.

Swords differ in shape and length. Tachi are very long, slim and have a strong curvature. Katana are shorter and not so curved. The length of the Wakazashi is under 60 cm. They are worn in the belt beside the sword. A sharp sword is a dangerous weapon and must be handled with care. To avoid injury, beginners should not practice with a real sword called Shinken, but use a replica called Iaito instead, which is made of soft metal and which is impossible to sharpen. After several years of training, I believe, it is worth using a real sword, because Nukitsuke and Noto must be practiced with more concentration. This will improve the mental and spiritual part of the training, which is important in sword art.

Tegatana, the sword hand: The curvature and shape of the Katana are no coincidence since both are essential for its effectiveness in sword combat. There is a reason why the blade is curved and has only one cutting edge and a blunt backside. This shape is a great advantage in combat. Find out why later in this book. The parts of the blade can be compared with the *empty hand* combat

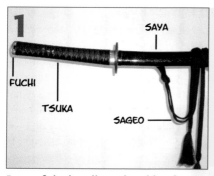

Parts of the handle and scabbard

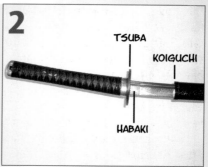

Parts between the blade and the handle

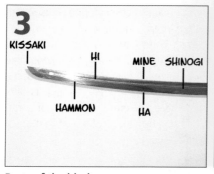

Parts of the blade

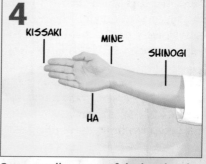

Corresponding parts of the hand and forearm

techniques. The blade resembles the forearm and the hand, as you can see in Figures 3 and 4. The Ha corresponds to the side of the little finger, the Mine to the side of the thumb and the inside and outside of the forearm to the Shinogi. The finger tips are used like the Kissaki, and the elbow must be bent a little in all the techniques. This is very important and you should keep that in mind. Always using the arm like the sword is a must if you want to perform the techniques the correct way.

3 The Dojo and etiquette

The Dojo: The Dojo is the location where people practice the Japanese martial arts. Today, in most cases this will most likely be a public sports center, and only seldom will you have the opportunity to practice in a private Dojo. Dojo does not only denote the location, but also the spiritual connection to a teacher or a style.

In the Dojo itself the Kamiza is the orientation point. The Kamiza side in the Dojo is called Shomen. In Aikido and Aikido Toho Iai there is a picture on the wall of MORIHEI UESHIBA, the founder of Aikido and NISHIO Sensei, the founder of Aikido Toho Iai.

In the Dojo community there is a teacher, experienced disciples and beginners. The teacher is called Sensei. The advanced pupils are called Yudansha, the beginners are called Mudansha. You will not become a Yudansha only by improving your ability. It is also necessary to strengthen your mind and soul according to the way of the warrior. A Yudansha always gives more to the Dojo than he takes. For him, the Dojo is much more than a sports center. It is a part of his life and the members are a part of his family.

Therefore all the members of the Dojo are connected in a Sempai and Kohei relationship. Everybody, even the teacher, is always a Sempai and a Kohei at the same time. The Sempai is the senior member, despite his physical skills or the degree he might have. The Kohei is the junior member. Even if he is more skilled and higher ranked than his senior, he has to respect him as long as he lives. The senior takes care of his junior and always tries to be a guide to him on his way of Budo.

Clothes: Everybody in the Dojo wears white training clothes called Keikogi. The left side of the jacket is crossed over the right side and fixed by a normal white belt used in Aikido. A special belt (Obi in Japanese) as is worn in Iaido is not deemed necessary. The pupil's belt is white. The master's belt is always black, no matter what rank he has.

In Aikido and Aikido Toho Iai, people wear the traditional Japanese pants of the Samurai, called Hakama. In most Dojos only the students who have mastered a black belt are allowed to wear the Hakama. I believe it is useful to wear them when

The picture shows the Hakama with the Gi and the belt

The official sign of Aikido Toho Iai

仁	Kindness
儀	Honor
礼	Courtesy
知	Wisdom
真	Truth
忠	Loyalty
考	Respect of parents

The seven folds of the Hakama, representing the seven virtues of the Samurai. Kindness, honor, courtesy, wisdom, truth, loyalty and respect of parents

practicing with the sword. Beginners should wear the Hakama in order to learn the correct movement in Aikido and Aikido Toho Iai as well as to understand the spiritual meaning of the seven folds of the Hakama, which represent the seven virtues of the Samurai. Its color should be black or blue, not white, since the latter is reserved for the Shinto priests only.

Aikido Toho Iai is the connecting, and to many people the invisible link between the art of sword combat and Aikido. For this reason you should always practice Aikido and Aikido Toho Iai together, including the partner forms with the wooden sword (Bokken) and stick (Jo), the Ken Tai Ken and Ken Tai Jo. The beginner should learn how to put on the Hakama from a senior since there are many ways to do so. These are not described in this book. Always treat the Hakama carefully and with respect. It symbolizes the seven virtues of the Samurai, which have to be accomplished. This is the main aim of martial arts training.

The Behavior in the Dojo: The first thing to do when entering the Dojo is to bow in the direction of the Kamiza. Sitting down in Seiza is not so common in Europe as it is in Japan. In Europe you are allowed to bow while standing. Outside the mat it is a good idea to wear Zori, Japanese slippers made out of rice straw, in order to keep the mats clean. You should always be calm and polite in the Dojo and watch the training carefully. You are not allowed to eat and drink or do anything other than training there. Before stepping onto the mat, you should slip out of the Zori, turn towards the Kamiza and bow again. If the training lesson has not started yet, it is advisable to start with Suburi or some stretching exercises. When the teacher steps onto the mat, the disciples sit down in a line, looking towards the Kamiza. In Japan, the highest ranked pupils normally sit on the right side.

Safety measures: For safety reasons beginners should not practice with a real sword. Injuries are common like cutting the hand or fingers while drawing the sword or when putting it back into the scabbard. Please remember that Bokken or Iaito are also dangerous weapons. Therefore, you should practise very carefully with them. It is important to have enough space between you and your partner. Never make a stroke in other peoples' direction, because the blade could break or slip out of the handle. Please check your sword before every training to avoid injuries caused by material defects.

4 The training lesson

The greeting prior to training

Carrying the sword in the Dojo

Showing respect to the Kamiza

Figure 1: In Aikido Toho Iai the training lesson begins with the formal bow to the founder of Aikido and to each other. You bow to the sword in an erect position after stepping onto the mat. You should hold the sword in the right hand with its backside facing forward to show that you are peaceable and do not intend to start a fight. It is not possible to draw the sword when carrying it in this manner.

Figure 2: First, everybody shows their respect to the Kamiza. The portaits of O Sensei, the founder of Aikido and NISHIO Sensei, the founder of Aikido Toho Iai, normally hang there on the wall. After that, the sword is put into the left hand where the scabbard is held below the Tsuba with the Mine facing towards the floor. The right hand covers both the handle and the left hand from above. Standing in an erect position with both feet together, everybody bows to the Shomen after the command 'Shomen Ni Rei' in Japanese.

Showing respect to the teacher   Showing respect to the sword

Figure 3: The next step is to show respect to the teacher by bowing to him after the command 'Mina San Rei', holding the sword in the same manner as when entering the Dojo.

Figure 4: After bowing to the teacher, the students show respect to their own sword by bowing to it as well. Standing straight, you should grasp the sword from behind with both hands and the hilt on the right. When hearing the command 'To Ni Rei' you should hold the sword about shoulder level, bow with a straight back until your forehead is about level with the sword. Make sure the Sageo is not hanging down but looped between the middle and the ring finger of the right hand instead.

Figure 5: Finally, you insert the scabbard under the bands of the Hakama. You should not look down while doing this. With the edge facing upwards, the end of the sheath (called the Kojiri) is placed on the left hip while holding the sword with both hands.

Inserting the sword into the belt

Tying the Sageo on the Hakama

The hilt must point straight towards the opponent in order to prevent him judging the length of the sword

Use your left thumb to insert the Kojiri into the belt only under the first winding. You should not do this at the hip but on the left side of your body between the navel and the hip. Push it through the belt underneath the cords of the Hakama with the right hand while pulling with the left hand.

Figure 6: The Sageo is placed over the scabbard from behind with the left hand and then tied underneath the belt on the right side. The sword should not sit too tight in the belt. It is advisable to loosen the belt a little before training.

Picture 7: In Aikido Toho Iai, the sword is placed in the belt straight and not diagonal, which is common in most other Iaido schools. The hilt is pointing in the direction of the aggressor. The length of the sword can no longer be judged, which is a great advantage.

Suburi - Basic exercises

When preparing for the lesson, you should start with some basic exercises, called Suburi. In general you should do Shomen Uchi, Yokomen Uchi, Kaesagiri Oroshi and Jodan No Tsuki left and right about ten times each.

How to practice the forms: The teacher shows the form three times from three different angles. After that the form will be practiced together with the teacher step by step. The Sensei counts the beginning of the form, speaking aloud the numbers of the respective step in Japanese. The end is always the same, first Seigan, secondly Chiburi and thirdly Osame. The method of Chiburi depends on the form itself.

Finishing the training lesson: To finish the lesson it is common to pay respect to the sword, to the teacher and to each other. First you draw the sword out of the Hakama without looking. Then you bow in the reverse sequence as you did at the beginning, first to the sword, then to the founder and at last to the teacher, saying "Domo Arigato Gozaimasu", which means "thank you very much for teaching me". Leaving the mat, you put the sword in the right hand, the Mine facing forward. On the edge of the mat you turn towards the Shomen and bow again, lifting the sword to shoulder height. After that you slip into your Zori and walk to the door. Then you turn again, bow and leave the Dojo walking backwards.

PART II
BASICS

1 Before the fight

1.1 Consciously and actively expecting the attack

Stand upright and relaxed with both feet together. Your knees are slightly bent. The heels are touching each other and are lifted up a little. Your weight is evenly distributed on both feet. The arms are hanging loosely to the sides of the body. You are looking straight ahead, never down or at the floor. Keep an eye on your opponent without fixating him. Just look loosely in his direction.

1.2 How to release the safety clip of the sword

Every form begins with a step left while releasing the safety clip of the sword. A good sword clips with the Habaki relatively firm in the scabbard. Therefore it is necessary to unlock it enabling you to draw it quickly and easily.

Figure 1: Using the knuckle of the index finger you can release the blade by pushing against the guard, moving it about an inch out of the scabbard. Simultaneously the thumb is used like a hook to prevent the blade from sliding out too far. The left index finger is on the Habaki between the guard and the scabbard. The sword is now ready to be drawn.

Figure 2: The first step is always a left step forward. During this movement the toes should not be raised. The foot glides above the floor. Your weight is transferred to the left foot and at the same time the right heel is lifted slightly. The upper part of the body should always be straight and relaxed. The left hand unlocks the sword. The thumb-side of the right hand is laid on the part of the Tsuka facing downward. The hand and wrist are protected by the hilt. At the same time the sword is slightly moved forward in the direction of the aggressor.

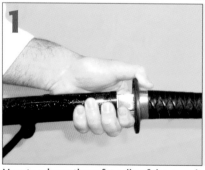

How to release the safety clip of the sword

The first step left

2 In sword combat with the opponent

2.1 How to deal with the attack

In Aikido Toho Iai it is not usual to wait until the enemy attacks. The idea is to move the very moment he moves. You step towards the opponent to settle the conflict, although he has raised his sword for cutting. When he strikes with Kiri Oroshi, you make a half step left or right turning about 45° to face the opponent. This movement is called Irimi, and it is very important to understand it. It is the basic movement in sword arts. Therefore it has to be practiced frequently to become familiar with it.

As in the principles of Sword Combat and Aikido, thinking of a spinning top helps a lot to gain insight into the principles of Irimi. You are the spinning top. The vertical axis of your body is the axis of rotation for movement. You won't need much impetus to be very quick. And your movements are not really big ones.

Since Aikido has been developed from sword combat, every Aikido technique also begins in the same manner with Irimi and Atemi. Irimi is a very special but simple movement. It enables the defender to reach a position from which he can strike and control the attacker in an instant only by a quick and small movement of the body.

Because it is only a half step with a small turn of the body, the movement is so quick that you can handle even the fastest attacks without being hit. Stepping to the outside the defender will enter the blind spot behind the attacker, called Ura. Stepping to the inside (called Omote), he will stay in front of the opponent.

Most people understand that the first movement will bring an advantage because you stay behind the attacker. The advantage of the second method is not so clear to see at first. But there is a blind spot in front of the opponent, too, and this is very important to know. Knowing that Irimi is always a half step to the side with a turn of about 45° towards the opponent, you will see that there are altogether four possibilities to move relative to the attacker, beginning from a right or left forward stance.

A   Making a half step forward
1   Reaching the outside position when the attack came straight
2   Reaching the inside position when the attack came from the side

B   Making a half step backward
3   Reaching the inside position when the attack came straight
4   Reaching the outside position when the attack came from the side

2.2 The entrance from the outside

Figure 3 and Figure 6: The picture shows the footwork when both opponents square off in a right forward stance. The attacker's feet are shown in black, the defender's in grey. The foot outline shows its position before taking a step.

Figure 4 and Figure 7: The first method is to leave the line of attack to the left. Dori makes a half step forward and puts his foot about a shoulderwidth to the left. This is just enough to bring Dori's head out of danger.

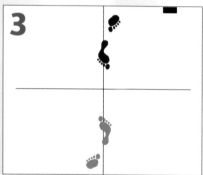

Right forward fighting stance

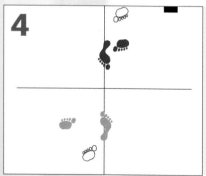

Half step forward to the left side

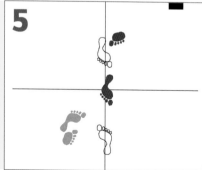

Turn about 45° to the right, feet together

This figure corresponds to Figure 3

This figure corresponds to Figure 4

This figure corresponds to Figure 5

Figure 5 and Figure 8:
With a turn to the right of about 45°, the right foot has to be pulled behind the left one, standing only on the ball of the foot. The weight is completely shifted to the left leg, leaning forward a little. Now the defender has completely left the line of attack and reached the blind spot behind the outside position of the opponent.

2.3 The entrance from the inside

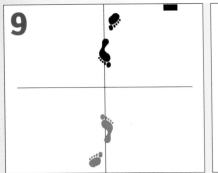

Right forward fighting stance

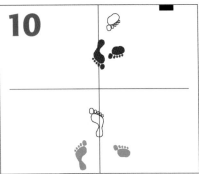

Half step backward with the right foot

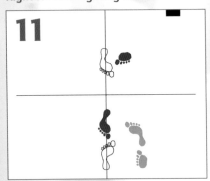

Turn about 45° to the left,
feet together

Figure 9 and Figure 12: The picture shows the same stance used in the outside Irimi when waiting for the attack.

Figure 10 and Figure 13: The second method to leave the line is to step backward to the right side, also with a half step. The foot is placed about a shoulderwidth from the left one, standing momentarily on the ball of the foot. Is is very important to point the toes towards the opponent. This is also just enough to move the head out of the line of danger when your opponent cuts.

The figure corresponds to Figure 9

The figure corresponds to Figure 10

The figure corresponds to Figure 11

Figure 11 and Figure 14: With a turn of the hips to the left of about 45°, the left foot has to be pulled just behind the right one. Make sure you step only on the ball of the foot. Your weight is completely shifted over the right leg with the whole body leaning forward a little. Now the defender has completely left the line of attack and reached the blind spot in front of the opponent. Movements are small but effective and distances may appear quite close but are sufficient.

2.4 Drawing the sword

Figure 15: The opponent's cut has to be caught with your own blade without blocking it. For a quick draw it is important to turn the Saya counterclockwise a little to the outside with the left hand. Doing so the right hand can grasp the handle naturally in the correct manner.

The method of drawing the sword depends on the form which is practiced. Be very careful to draw the blade completely out of the scabbard before changing the direction of the sword. To do so the sword has to be drawn straight forward while shifting the left hip back as far as possible. This movement is not easy, especially when beginners are using a long sword. Pulling the sword to the right side before the point has left the scabbard, it is possible to break it open with the Iaito. With a real sword you may cut the Saya and along with it all the fingers of your left hand. Therefore a beginner should never practice with a sharp blade. The danger should be taken seriously and not underestimated as stories have been told about this kind of injury that had in fact happened in Japanese sword schools of today.

Figure 16: When actively using your own blade for dealing with the opponent's cut, it is very important to be able to catch the cutting edge of the attacker with the tough backside of your blade to avoid chips in your own cutting edge or even the breaking of the sword. Both can cost your life in a real combat.

When dealing with a cut, the whole body has to avoid the path of the blade. Therefore it is important to show only the smallest part of the body when the opponent attacks, which can be achieved by turning the shoulder and the hip towards the opponent. Never move only the upper part of your body while standing still with your feet. Take care to be always at an erect position while moving. The acceleration of the sword must come from the legs and hips. The backside of the blade catching the cut should also be held at a small angle to the sword of the opponent. It is completely wrong to block the cut. Lead the blade away to the side instead. This will absorb the energy of the cut, protect your own sword and throw the opponent off balance by virtue of his own impetus.

15

Drawing the sword

16

When catching the cut of the opponent the backside of the blade has to be turned to the outside

2.5 The counterattack

After catching the oppponent's cut there are different possibilities like straight, diagonal or horizontal cuts to counter the attack. They can be divided up into cuts at the upper level, the middle section and the lower level. The upper level, called Jodan, extends from the skull to the shoulders. The middle section extends from the shoulders to the hips and is called Chudan. The lower level is named Gedan and extends from the hips to the feet. Downward cuts are called Kiri Oroshi, and those upwards Kiriage. Thrusts (called Tsuki) to the throat are performed by holding the blade straight and those to the heart are performed by holding the blade parallel to the ground. Otherwise it would not be possible to penetrate the chest between the ribs. It is worth exercising these techniques, which are called Suburi (or basic exercises) for about ten minutes before the training lesson starts.

2.6 Fundamentals of cutting

The different schools of swordsmanship are sometimes considerably different in the way they execute the cut. The sword has originally been made for cutting, because cutting is much more effective than thrusting. Firstly, because you can avoid a thrust easier than a cut, and secondly a cut will cause deeper wounds and more loss of blood than a thrust. But the most important thing is that in combat with many opponents cutting is the only way and you survive by whirling the sword through the crowd of enemies disabling the greatest number possible with the first strike.

It is natural that particularly the beginner wastes a lot of energy when trying to cause a loud and impressive sound. But it is much more important to learn the cut in the correct manner. Therefore it is much better to perform it very slowly when beginning. Please keep in mind the following points:

The acceleration of the blade, especially the point, must come from the left hand. It is thus important to keep the elbows held down deep. The left hand draws the handle straight downward in the center line of the body while the right hand pushes it forward and gives the cut its proper direction. In order to reach the full distance it is necessary to extend both arms as far as possible with the feeling of throwing the sword forward. After the point has reached the maximum distance it must be drawn back only by using the left hand until the end of the handle stops about two inches in front of the navel.

In ancient times people used to say that the sword has to be held like a bird. Not too firm, which would crush it to death, and not to lightly, giving it the

Bad example, the extended arm allows you to be hit on the wrist

Correct example, drawing the wrist back prevents you from being cut

When trying to hit the opponent with the point of the sword, he is able to avoid the cut by simply stepping back

Touching the body with the middle of the blade for a proper cut

Causing deep wounds as a consequence of putting pressure on the cutting edge with the right hand

Proper grip with the right hand

opportunity to fly away. To perform the cut in the described manner has a great advantage in a life and death situation. You must keep in mind that in those times even a small wound could cause a cruel death by infection, because there was no medicine like there is nowadays. Therefore it was very important to prevent being wounded anywhere at all. If your cut missed its target and your arms were extended as it is taught in most other schools, especially your right wrist was in danger of being cut by the opponent. Drawing the sword back to your navel will give you some more space to bring your wrist out of the range of the opponent's blade.

When cutting the air while training, you can feel that drawing the handle back with the left hand helps you to stop the blade without shaking it because you do not need the right hand for stopping. Using the right hand to stop the cut is completely wrong.

Since the sword has been made for cutting, it should be drawn along the full length of the blade and with pressure applied on the body when cutting. To put a maximum of pressure on the cutting edge, it is important to put maximum weight on top of the handle with the index finger. Therefore the right hand has to be turned a little counterclockwise to the inside. The pressure of the index finger while drawing back with the left hand causes the desired effect of the cut. When cutting in this manner it is not possible to use the right hand for stopping the sword.

In close combat fighting it is useful to put the left hand on the blunt backside to apply pressure on the cutting edge while drawing the sword back with the right hand.

The speed of the cutting blade is tremendous, almost like a bullet. Despite this a skilled fighter can avoid getting hit by simply stepping back when the cut is planned too short. For this reason and for causing deep wounds the blade should touch the body, not with the end of the blade, but about the middle of the edge. To cut in this manner the body has to move first and only then does the sword follow as can be read in the "Gorin No Sho" by Miyamoto Musashi.

In order to avoid losing the balance when missing the target and to compensate for the momentum of the cut, a movement in the opposite direction is necessary. This is created by stepping back with the left leg and shifting the body weight downward. The momentum of the sword and the counter movement of the body will keep the strongly bent right knee fixed stiff, help to keep the upper body erect and allow a clean cut to be made without shaking.

Try to cut the exposed and soft areas of the body like the side of the neck, the downward side of the forearm, the hip and the inside of the thighs, where vital arteries are located. The cut should always end horizontally because it allows you to follow your opponent with a thrust without wasting any time that would be needed to lift it up again.

2.7 Shomen Uchi: The straight downward cut

Figure 23: Shomen Uchi is a straight downward cut in the centerline of the body beginning from the skull (Jodan No Kamae).

Figure 24: For maximum range you should fully extend the arms while cutting. The stance used is called Zenkutsu Tachi.

Figure 25: Finishing the cut parallel to the ground makes it possible to thrust after the cut without wasting any time.

Shomen Uchi, beginning from Jodan No Kamae

Shomen Uchi in the middle phase

Finish the cut always with the blade parallel to the ground

2.8 Kaesagiri Oroshi: The diagonal cut

Figure 26: The diagonal downward cut, called Kaesagiri Oroshi, also starts from the middle of the skull (Jodan No Kamae).

Figure 27: The cut is driven from your opponent's shoulder to his opposite hip and is finished with the end of the handle stopping about two inches in the front of the lower abdomen.

Figure 28: Drawing the Katana back will stop the blade horizontally automatically. Since the cut is diagonal, the sword has to be pulled to the opposite hip.

Kaesagiri, beginning from
Jodan No Kamae

Kaesagiri, middle phase

Finish the Kaesagiri always parallel to the ground

2.9 Yokomen Uchi: The cut to the neck

Figure 29: Yokomen Uchi is different to Kaesagiri Oroshi because it hits the temple or the side of the neck. Therefore, the cut is thrown much more in a forward direction and stopped at the level of the head, feet closed for maximum range.

Yokomen Uchi, a cut to the neck

2.10 Kiriage: The upward cut

Figure 30: Kiriage, a diagonal upward cut, is used to counter downward cuts like Shomen Uchi from Jodan No Kamae. The cut drives from the hip to the opposite shoulder. Preparing the cut it is necessary to turn the edge towards the enemy. When performing Kiriage from the right to the left, the sword is on the right side and the left hand turns the handle. When performing it from the left to the right, the sword is on the left side and the right hand is turning the handle.

Figure 31: In this figure you can clearly see how to hold the sword after finishing a cut from the right hip to the left shoulder of the opponent. The power comes from the hip, shifting the body weight from the left to the right. The arms and shoulders are completely relaxed while standing in a deep Kibadachi.

Preparing for Kiriage

Kiriage after finishing the cut

2.11 Do Uchi: The horizontal cut

Figure 32: Do Uchi is a horizontal cut at hip level where the armor of the Samurai used to be weak. You should start with the blade on the inside of your left elbow.

Figure 33: Standing in a deep Kibadachi, you cut horizontally from the left to the right side. It is important not to swing the blade too much to the right. It should be stopped exactly at your right hip.

Preparing for Do Uchi

Do Uchi after finishing the cut

2.12   Tsuki: The straight thrust

Figure 34: Start with the Tsuki holding the sword in Seigan. The point is directed towards the left eye of the opponent while standing in Zenkutsu Tachi, the common forward stance.

Figure 35: Pulling the back foot to the front foot, you can close the distance without having to fear that it might be noticed by the opponent. After that you perform the thrust with the power of the hip pushing forward with the backward leg.

Figure 36: To reach the maximum range it is very important to extend your arms as far as possible. Simultaneously you make a large forward step with your front leg and keep the upper body relaxed and erect.

Seigan is used as the fighting position

First you should close the distance or bridge the gap between you and your opponent with the back foot coming to the front and the latter making a forward step. The akama is used to conceal this almost invisible bridging of the gap

Figure 37: After the opponent has been hit, the sword must be pulled back in an instant, because in life and death combat, taking too much time could cost the Samurai his life. The sword must be pulled back with the left hand while you create a momentum by pulling the rear leg towards the front leg. This is necessary to keep the center stable. Thrusting to the throat allows you to hold the blade in a normal manner, but if you thrust to the chest you have to turn the blade horizontally with the backside towards your body, otherwise it would not be feasible to penetrate your opponent's ribcage.

The straight thrust to the throat

Pulling the sword back from the opponent's body

3   The fight is over

3.1 Controlling the opponent

3.1.1 Seigan: The on guard position

After the last strike, maybe a cut, or a thrust, you stand in the on guard position called Seigan. In this position you should relax and take your time to rebuild a calm mind while controlling the opponent in a proper way. From this position you can hit the opponent lying on the floor easily with a cut, or ward off another attack. Seigan is one of the most important positions and worth being studied well. It is also called the position of the clear eyes.

Seigan, the position of the clear eyes

Figure 1: One of the most important positions is called Seigan. The basis of it is Zenkutsu Tachi, described here as the right forward stance.

When performing Zenkutsu Tachi the right knee is bent almost 90° and Dori stands with legs about shoulder width apart and in a deep Kibadachi. The right knee and the right foot are facing inward. The body weight rests almost completely on the front leg. The left leg is stretched fully out. The left heel is lifted a little. The toes point forward. Head, back and the rear leg form a straight line. This helps to stand in a line, but nevertheless very stable, offering as little body surface as possible to a potential attacker. It is important to keep the left leg stretched, otherwise the stance would be quite weakened. The upper body is held erect. Shoulders and arms are completely relaxed hanging by the side of the body. The hips are held sideways and do not point forward. The lower body and the legs are held tensed. The mind concentrates on Dori's own Hara, a point about the width of one hand below the navel.

The sword is held with the handle about two inches in front of the lower belly. The hands are slightly turned inward while at the same time holding the hilt not too firmly. The Kissaki is directed towards the opponent's left eye, protecting the right wrist. You should not fix your gaze on anything but watch all around you. The position of the sword, the posture of the body together with the mental attitude will help you to perform Seigan, called the position of the clear eyes.

3.1.2 Jodan No Kamae: The upper level position

Figure 2: All downward cuts start from Jodan No Kamae, even if they are straight like Shomen Uchi or diagonal like Yokomen Uchi or Kaesagiri Oroshi. It is important to keep in mind that every cut starts from the center of the skull. It is also important to keep the elbows deep without lifting them up because the sword is accelerated by pulling the left elbow straight downward in the centerline. The right elbow is lifted a little since the right hand has to support the sword from behind.

3.1.3 Gedan No Kamae: The lower level position

Figure 3: Gedan No Kamae is used for cuts from below as well as for controlling the opponent lying on the ground. If you want to cut upward, the cutting edge must be directed upward. For controlling the opponent lying on the floor hold the sword in a normal manner with the cutting edge facing downward.

Jodan No Kamae,
the upper level position

Gedan No Kamae,
the lower level position

3.1.4 Shira Seigan:
The horizontal sword
position

Figure 4: Shira Seigan is used to initiate the performance of the second form of Chiburi. Because in this form the sword has to rotate some complete 360°, it is necessary to hold it horizontally to the ground.

Shira Seigan,
holding the blade horizontally

3.1.5 Shin No Kamae:
The position to
threaten the heart of
the opponent

Figure 5: In Shin No Kamae the tip of the sword is pointing towards the heart of your opponent while the blade protects Dori's upper body at the same time. Hold the sword using your right hand in front of your belly, the cutting edge facing upward. The right hand grasps the handle from above, the left hand from below. Mine lies on Dori's lower arm. Stand in an upright position with your body erect but still relaxed in a deep Kibadachi. Out of this posture it is possible to make an upward cut or to thrust in the direction of your opponent.

Shin No Kamae, the position to
threaten the heart of the opponent

3.1.6 Waki Gedan No Kamae: The second lower level position

Figure 6: The body position of Waki Gedan No Kamae is the forward stance Zenkutsu Tachi. The sword is held above the right knee with the cutting edge directed diagonally upward. You can launch a Kiriage without moving your body.

3.1.7 Zenkutsu Tachi: The forward stance

Figures 7 – 8: Zenkutsu Tachi, the forward stance is one of the most basic positions in martial arts. However, it is common to find people perform it the wrong way. It is often used in Aikido Toho Iai, but not in Aikido. Since in Aikido quick movement is the basis, you cannot stay in a stiff, immobile or deep stance.

Waki Gedan No Kamae, holding the sword at the side, with the edge facing upward

But in sword art when the fight is over there is a moment for concentration and only then do you stay in Zenkutsu Tachi to perform Seigan. By holding a sword in the correct way when practicing, you will feel how to take up the right position, which you cannot feel when you try to perform the forward stance without it. Your sword will show you how to do it in the correct manner.

Zenkutsu Tachi, the forward stance

Zenkutsu Tachi, seen from a different angle

3.1.8 Kake Tachi: The crossed feet position

Figure 9: Kake Tachi is a position used when crossing over the feet or turning the body. It is very important to keep the body erect when performing this position. Please note that it is not a stance in the broader sense but simply a position, used only for a split second while shifting from one position to the other. Nevertheless you should practice it slowly when beginning.

Kake Tachi, the position when crossing the feet or turning the body

It will improve the power of your legs and hips tremendously because you have to bend your knees while standing on your front leg. The foot of your front leg is turned with the toes 90° outwards, standing flat on the floor. The rear leg is also bent and the knee pushes into the calf of the forward leg for balance, while at the same time you lift the heel a little.

3.2 Shaking the blood from the blade

Following on from Seigan, the shaking of the blood from the blade called Chiburi is carried out. Besides removing the blood, the action is also used to control the opponent, who lies on the ground in front of you, until you can be sure that there is no more danger. The form of the Chiburi used depends on the sword form that is practiced. Up to the form Kawashi Tsuki the first form of the Chiburi is always used. It is stems from Eishin Ryu.

From Tsukekomi to Sanpo the second form is used which stems from Tenshin Shoden Katori Shinto Ryu. Only in Shiho and Nukiawase a special form of Chiburi is performed, stemming from Suio Ryu. In the last two forms Todome and Suemonogiri you will use the first form again, its style stems from Eishin Ryu.

3.2.1 The first form of Chiburi

Figures 1 – 2: The first form of the blood removal stems from the Eishin Ryu. It is performed after Seigan. The right hand grasps the handle from the outside. This allows you to relax your wrist while performing the Chiburi. To shake the blood from the blade cut horizontally to the outside. Simultaneously the left hand is placed on the Obi where it crosses the Saya. Where you stop it the blade has to be held with the point a little bit downward and to the inside. The guard is on the level of the hip beside your right knee. Please make sure that the arm is slightly bent and the shoulder is completely relaxed. From this position you can launch a thrust to the opponent in an instant without moving your body.

The first form of Chiburi as seen from the front

The first form of Chiburi as seen sideways

3.2.2 The second form of Chiburi

Figure 3: The second form of the Chiburi stems from the Tenshin Shoden Katori Shinto Ryu. It is used in the forms from Tsukekomi to Sanpo. From Seigan you shift the sword very slowly into a horizontal position called Shira Seigan. The handle stops about one inch in front of your lower belly. The left hand grasps it in a relaxed manner while the right hand takes the lower rim of the handle only with the end of the fingers, which are formed like a claw.

Figure 4: For this kind of Chiburi a lot of practice is required. The sword rotates completely 360° in the left hand and must be stopped exactly at the right moment. Good timing is the watchword here. Therefore the left hand has to relax allowing the handle to move freely, but not too much. Take care not to drop it. The momentum of the rotation is created by the right hand pulling it from the Shira Seigan position quickly towards your left shoulder.

Figure 5: After the complete rotation, the blade has to be stopped exactly at the right moment. Then the right hand knocks the handle. Both the rotating motion and knocking shake the blood from the blade.

Figure 6: The figure shows a simple method for learning this Chiburi without the danger of damaging your sword. Sitting on your knees while performing it minimizes any damage in case you accidentally let your sword fall.

How to hold the sword when performing the second Chiburi

The full 360° rotation of the sword when performing the second Chiburi

Holding the sword after the rotation of the blade

A way of learning the Chiburi without endangering your sword

3.2.3   The third form of Chiburi

Figure 7: The third form of blood removal is used only in one single form called Shiho. From Seigan you let the sword sink into the Gedan No Kamae position.

Figure 8: From this position you pull the sword up powerfully towards your left shoulder. The blade is held diagonally, pointing towards the opponent, who lies on the ground at your right side. Notice that the left hand is pulling while the right hand supports the handle from below.

The beginning of the third form of the Chiburi

Finishing the third form of the Chiburi

3.2.4   The fourth form of Chiburi

Figure 9: The fourth form of Chiburi is used only in the form called Nukiawase, starting from Gedan No Kamae.

Figure 10: The right hand grasps the handle from above with the thumb pointing towards your own body. This method of grasping is called Gyaku Te.

Figure 11: The right forearm is twisted downwards from the elbow. This will turn the cutting edge of the blade facing upward with the Kissaki pointing towards the opponent. Then you put your left hand on the end of the handle in order to thrust towards him if need should be.

Figure 12: After that the left hand lets go of the Tsuka. The left forearm has to be bent some 90° from the elbow with the palm facing downward. Then you strike the backside of your left hand on the right forearm from below in order to shake the blood from the blade.

The beginning of the fourth form of the Chiburi

Grasping the handle with Gyaku Te

How to threaten the opponent

Shaking the blood from the blade

4 Finishing the form

4.1 Resheathing the sword

After shaking off the blood you resheathe the sword. This is called the Noto. When performing the Noto you must take care when resheathing the blade as well as moving the scabbard with the left hand, which is called Sayabiki action. The two movements, performed at the same time, do the trick.

4.1.1 The first form of the Noto

Up to the form Kawashi Tsuki the first form of the Noto is used when resheathing the sword. This form stems from the Eishin Ryu.

Figure 1: Resheathing the sword starts by aligning it up with the scabbard, an action called Sayabiki. When performing Sayabiki the left hand slides from the belt to the opening of the scabbard, which is called the Koiguchi.

Figure 2: Now grasp the end of the scabbard and pull it until it reaches the center of your lower belly. Turn it to the outside until it is horizontal and you can place the rim, where the cutting edge is located, into the skin fold between your thumb and index finger. The scabbard is pushed back and then pulled straight forward again.

The position of the hand and the sword when starting Noto

The position of the scabbard in front of the center of the lower abdomen

How to put the backside of the blade on the scabbard

Leading the tip of the blade into the opening of the scabbard

Pushing the scabbard over the blade

Resheathing the blade

Sliding along the top of the handle to its end

Securing the sword

Figure 3: The blunt backside of the blade makes contact with the scabbard about the middle of the Mine.

Figure 4: The handle of the sword is directed straight forward and the cutting edge of the blade faces upward. Make sure to draw the sword straight forward until the tip falls into the opening of the scabbard without touching your hand. Never circle the handle in front of your body.

Figure 5: After that, push the scabbard very slowly over the blade until two parts of it are resheathed. The last part of the blade has to be pushed into the Saya without causing any noise. At the end, the index finger lies between the guard and the scabbard while the thumb forms a hook to secure the sword at the Tsuba.

Figure 6: Now the sword has to be pushed back into the belt until the guard is placed about two inches in front of the center of the lower abdomen. The right hand lies on top of the handle, prepared to draw the sword again if need should be.

Figure 7: If you are sure that there isn't any threat left from your opponent or some other enemy around you, slide with your right hand very slowly along the top of the handle towards its end.

Figure 8: Then push the sword into the scabbard with your right hand to secure it. It is now not possible to draw it until the safety clip has been released again.

4.1.2 The second form of the Noto

After knocking the handle in the second form of the Chiburi, the second form of resheathing the sword begins.

This kind of the Noto is used in the forms Tsukekomi, Tsume and Sanpo. It stems from the Tenshin Shoden Katori Shinto Ryu.

Placing the backside of the blade on the left shoulder

Changing the grip on the handle

Figures 9 – 10: After the Chiburi, put the backside of the sword onto your left shoulder while holding the handle in the normal way. The right hand releases the grip and grasps the handle from below with the thumb pointing towards the opposite side of the body.

Figure 11: The resheathing of the blade starts again with the correct placement of the scabbard, called Sayabiki. When performing Sayabiki the left hand slides from the belt to the opening of the scabbard (Koiguchi in Japanese). Now grasp the end of the scabbard and pull it until it reaches the center of your lower belly. There turn it to the outside until it is horizontal and you can place the rim, where the cutting edge is located, into the skin fold between your thumb and index finger. The scabbard is pushed back and then pulled straight forward again. The blunt backside of the blade (Mine) touches the scabbard (Saya) near the Tsuba.

Figure 12: The handle of the sword is directed straight forward and the cutting edge of the blade faces upward. Be sure to draw the sword straight forward until the tip falls into the opening of the scabbard without touching your hand. Never circle the hilt in front of your body.

Putting the Mine on the Saya

Leading the tip of the blade into the scabbard

Pushing the scabbard forward

Securing the sword

Finishing the second form of the Noto

Figure 13: After that the scabbard is pushed over the blade about two thirds of its length. The the rest of the blade has to be pushed into the Saya very slowly and should be secured with light pressure.

Figures 14 – 15: Note that you have to pull the forward foot back to the rear foot. Closing the feet and securing the sword should take place at the same time. In this form securing the sword immediately after resheathing is possible because you move away from the opponent.

4.1.3 The third form of the Noto

The third form of the Noto is used only in the form Shiho. It stems from the Suio Ryu.

Figure 16: The Chiburi ends holding the sword diagonally in front of the body, pointing to the right side. The third form of the Noto begins again with the correct placement of the Saya, the Sayabiki. The left hand slides from the belt to the opening of the scabbard (Koiguchi in Japanese). Now grasp the end of the scabbard and pull it until it reaches the center of your lower belly. Turn it to the outside until it is horizontal and you can place the rim, where the cutting edge is located, into the skin fold between your thumb and index finger. Then the scabbard is pushed back again .

Figure 17: Swing the sword with your right hand with the cutting edge facing upward and place the blunt backside about its middle section on the Koiguchi. Now you must draw the sword straight forward until the point falls into the opening of the Saya without touching your hand. Please avoid circling the hilt in front of your body.

Figures 18 – 19: Then push the scabbard very slowly over the blade until two thirds of it are resheathed. The remaining part of the blade has to be pushed into the Saya without causing any noise. At the end, the index finger lies between the guard and the scabbard while the thumb forms a hook to secure the sword at the Tsuba.

Figure 20: Now the sword is pushed back into the belt until the guard is placed about two inches in front of the center of your lower abdomen. The right hand holds the Tsuka Gyaku Te, ready to draw the sword again if need should be. If you are sure that there isn't any threat left from the opponent or some other enemy around you, slide your right hand very slowly along the underside of the handle towards its end. Then push the sword into the scabbard with your right hand to secure it. It is now not possible to draw it until the safety clip has been released again.

How to grasp the Saya

Placing the backside of the blade on the scabbard

Resheathing the sword

Securing the sword

Finishing the third form of the Noto

4.1.4 The fourth form of the Noto

The fourth method of the Noto is used only in the form Nukiawase. It also stems from the Suio Ryu.

Figure 21: After the Chiburi you hold the sword horizontally in front of your lower abdomen with the tip facing towards the left side. The cutting edge must be directed away from the body. Lay the end of the blade on the left index finger and support it with pressure on the handle from your right thumb.

Figures 22 and 23: The left hand grasps the scabbard at its end and leads it to the tip of the blade. Then carefully lead the Kissaki into the Saya and push the blade very slowly into it in order to avoid injury.

Placing the blade horizontally on the left hand

Leading the tip into the scabbard

Pushing the scabbard forward two thirds of the length of the blade

Resheathing the sword completely and securing it

Figure 24: To finish the Noto draw the right foot back to the left when the blade is resheathed about two thirds of its length. Closing the feet and securing the sword should take place at the same time.

4.2 After combat with the sword

To finish the form lift your body upright, pushing up from the knees. Standing in a completely natural and relaxed position you are ready to perform the next sword form.

PART III
THE SWORD FORMS

1 Shohatto Maegiri

Meaning of the form Shohatto Maegiri: The first of the forms described in this book is Shohatto Maegiri, which means to start the sword exercise and cut forward. There is no Aikido technique connected to this form.

The aggressor is stopped by a cut to his throat before he can draw his sword. But because he was not hit, he steps back and is followed by the defender executing a straight downward cut, called Shomen Uchi. The form stresses the basic movements, the sword drawing, the cutting forward and the mental preparation which is necessary for good sword exercise. The form clearly shows that the best way to defend yourself when you find your life in danger is to stop the aggressor the very moment he starts his attack. To hesitate means to lose your life.

Cutting to the throat

Following up with Shomen Uchi

Controlling the aggressor

Waiting for the opponent in a natural on guard stance

Make a step forward to the left while releasing the sword catch

PERFORMING THE SHOHATTO MAEGIRI FORM

Figure 4: Stand upright and relaxed with both feet together. Your knees are slightly bent. The heels are touching each other and are lifted up a little. Your weight is evenly distributed on both feet. The arms are hanging loosely on the sides of the body. You are looking straight ahead, never down or at the floor. Keep an eye on your opponent without fixating him. Just look loosely in his direction.

Figure 5: The first step is always a step forward to the left. During this movement the toes should not be raised. The foot glides above the floor. Your weight is shifted onto the left foot and at the same time the right heel is lifted slightly. The upper part of the body should always be straight and relaxed. The left hand unlocks the sword. The thumb-side of the right hand is laid on the part of the Tsuka facing downward. The hand and wrist are protected by the hilt. At the same time the sword is slightly moved forward in the direction of the aggressor.

Make a second step with your right foot and grasp the sword

Draw the blade until only the tip is left inside the scabbard while making the third step with the left foot

Figure 6: After that make a right forward step. The left hand turns the sword about 45° counterclockwise to the outside. This enables the right hand to grasp the handle naturally.

Figure 7: Make the third left forward step. It is a little longer than the previous two. With this step you draw the blade until only the tip is left inside the scabbard. Be sure to turn the scabbard 90° to the outside just before the tip of the sword leaves the Saya. If you turn it too early a sharp sword will cut the scabbard. This may cause serious injury to your left hand.

Cut towards the throat while making the fourth step right

Make a fifth step left while preparing for Shomen Uchi

Figure 8: Then make the fourth step right. It is the longest and leads to the right forward stance called Zenkutsu Tachi. With this step forward you should draw the blade completely and cut towards the opponent's throat. Be sure not to swing your sword too much to the outside. The tip should always remain on the centerline. Also watch your posture. The right arm and shoulder have to be relaxed with the elbow slightly bent. Make sure not to cramp your wrist. While drawing the sword turn your left hip back as much as possible and draw the Saya back. This makes it easy to draw even a long sword without any problems.

Figure 9: With the fifth step you pull the left foot to the right. Simultaneously you lift the sword over your head as if thrusting it into the sky and perform Jodan No Kamae. The left hand draws the scabbard in front of your lower abdomen. The three movements, stepping, lifting the sword and drawing the scabbard should be performed at the same time.

Figure 10: In Jodan No Kamae you should hold the sword in a 45° angle. Make sure to keep your elbows down. Keep them deep and close to your body. It is

Start of the Shomen Uchi

Finish of the Shomen Uchi

important that you waste no time between the cut to the throat and the Shomen Uchi downward cut so that your opponent has no chance to counter.

Figure 11: The downward cut has to be launched with a big forward step to make it tremendously powerful. To stop the momentum of the body weight you have to use Zenkutsu Tachi. The sword must be accelerated only with your left hand, extending the arms for maximum range. After that you draw the sword back again only with the left hand until the end of the handle stops about two inches in front of the lower abdomen. The blade has to be exactly parallel to the floor. Throwing the sword forward and drawing it back creates an ellipsoid curve of the tip, which is the basis of a correct cut. Be sure not to strike out like when using an axe. While cutting, the right hand should be completely relaxed.

It is used only to give direction to the cut. Remember to always keep the upper body erect. Do not lean forward while cutting. From the beginning, up to this step the speed of the actions should increase continuously. Do not forget that the aggressor was surprised by the counterattack and pushed back so that he is no longer able to defend himself.

Step right back, perform Jodan No Kamae   Step left back and perform Seigan

Figure 12: Now the fight is over. The opponent is lying struck down on the floor. You can now take your time. From now on every movement is performed very slowly and in a relaxed manner. From Zenkutsu Tachi, step back to a natural posture and lift the sword slowly over your head to Jodan No Kamae. Keep the elbows deep. Do not turn your hips. Always watch the opponent on the ground with keen eyes. He might still be stirring.

Figure 13: Now perform Seigan, described in detail in the Chapter on the "Basics" 3.1.1, starting from page 40.

Figure 14: The figure shows the first Chiburi, completely described in Chapter 3.2.1, on page 45. The form stems from the Eishin Ryu.

Figure 15: The figure shows the first Noto. It is described in Chapter 4.1.1 on page 49. Place the blunt backside of the blade on the scabbard.

Figure 16: Leading the tip of the blade into the Koiguchi of the Saya.

Figure 17: Push the scabbard over the blade until only about two thirds of its length are covered.

Perform Chiburi, its style stems from Eishin Ryu

Place the sword on the Saya

Lead the tip of the blade into the scabbard

Push the scabbard over the blade until about two thirds of its length are covered

Resheathe the sword completely   Secure the blade

Finish the form in a relaxed position

Figure 18: Push the blade completely into the scabbard and then push both into the belt until only about two inches remain between your lower abdomen and the guard.

Figure 19: The right hand, holding the handle, slides slowly to its end and secures the sword by pushing it into the scabbard. Now the Habaki clips in the Koiguchi and the blade is safe. First align the sword in the belt and then pull the left foot to the right.

Figure 20: To finish the form stand up straight from the knees. Standing in a completely natural and relaxed posture you are ready to perform the next sword form.

The connection to Aikido: The form Shohatto Maegiri is easily integrated and worth the trouble of performing it several times at the beginning of every training lesson. It is a simple technique and serves to give mainly mental and spiritual exercise. Therefore you should concentrate on the basics of sword fighting while performing it. Determination, speed and the ability to focus your power with optimal timing is the main goal, while being completely relaxed in body and mind at the same time. Therefore it is important to imagine a life and death situation in your mind's eye when training. You should not look at the floor while performing this form. Throughout the action you must focus on an imaginary opponent until he is beaten. Improvement of this ability is also important for empty hand combat in Aikido since most street fights are decided in the mind before action has had time to evolve.

2 Ukenagashi

Meaning of the form Ukenagashi: The second sword form described in this book is named Ukenagashi, which means to protect yourself by turning your body to the side. In Aikido the corresponding form is Ai Hanmi or Shomen Uchi No Ikkyo Omote.

The cut of the opponent must be caught with the blunt backside of the blade. Simultaneously you make a half step to the side and turn your body to the left in order to leave the line of attack. You finish the opponent with a diagonal downward cut from his left shoulder to his right hip.

Catching the cut of the opponent

Leaving the line of attack

Finishing the opponent with Kaesagiri Oroshi

Waiting for the opponent in a natural stance

Make a step forward to the left while releasing the sword catch

PERFORMING THE UKENAGASHI FORM

Figure 4: Stand upright and relaxed with both feet together. Your knees are slightly bent. The heels are touching each other and are lifted up a little. Your weight is evenly distributed on both feet. The arms are hanging loosely on the sides of the body. You are looking straight ahead, never down or at the floor. Keep an eye on your opponent without fixating him. Just look loosely in his direction.

Figure 5: The first step is always a step forward to the left. During this movement the toes should not be raised. The foot glides above the floor. Your weight is transferred to the left foot and at the same time the right heel is lifted slightly. The upper part of the body should always be straight and relaxed. The left hand unlocks the sword. The thumb-side of the right hand is laid on the part of the Tsuka facing downward. The hand and wrist are protected by the hilt. At the same time the sword is slightly moved forward in the direction of the aggressor.

Make a second step to the right with Irimi

Turn to the left, draw your sword and protect yourself

Figure 6: The figure shows the outside Irimi. It is comprehensively described in Chapter 2.2, on page 26. Make a half step forward to the right, the toes pointing inward. The hips and the upper body turn about 45° to the left in order to avoid getting hit. Make sure not to lean forward.

The left hand draws the Saya in front of the lower abdomen, while turning it counterclockwise to the outside. The right hand grasps the handle from below after bending the wrist over the Tsuka. This is very important because it protects the wrist from the opponent's sword.

Figure 7: Turn sharply to the left and place the left foot alongside the right one. Make sure that the silhouette of your body towards your opponent is very small. The Saya must be pulled back as far as possible and directed upward to facilitate the release of the blade. While drawing the sword both hands should be turned with

8

Make a third step with the left foot
and lift the sword as if thrusting it in
to the sky

9

Start the Kaesagiri

the palm facing upward at the same time. This allows the blade to slide out of the scabbard on its blunt backside which is very important when training with a real Katana. The opponent's cut will be caught with the Mine, not with the cutting edge. It slides to the side and this causes the opponent to lose his balance throughout the impetus.

Figure 8: After defending the attack you take a large step forward left into Zenkutsu Tachi. Pull the right foot to the centerline and lift the heel up. Keep your hip straight and draw the scabbard in front of your lower abdomen. Make sure that your right knee is straight and not bent. Lift the sword over your head into Jodan No Kamae. All steps should flow one into the next.

Figure 9: Now grasp the handle with both hands and perform Kaesagiri Oroshi.

The figure shows Kaesagiri in its middle phase

Finish of the Kaesagiri

Figure 10: The cut is drawn from the right shoulder of the aggressor to his left hip. The power for acceleration comes from the left hand only. The right hand grasps the handle from above, gives direction to the blade and supports it by putting pressure on the edge while cutting. To reach maximum range, both arms should be extended and are then drawn back to the belly. Cutting in this manner will not blunt the cut.

Figure 11: Drawing the sword back with the left hand will halt the cut without the need for any further effort, at least not from the right hand in particular. The impetus alone is sufficient. The blade will stop exactly parallel to the ground. Up to this step, defense and counterattack alternate quickly without stopping. Now the opponent is hit and 'wounded', lying on the ground. From now on every step should be performed very slowly and relaxedly.

Take a step back left to Seigan

Perform Chiburi, its style stems from Eishin Ryu

Figure 12: Now perform Seigan, described in detail in the Chapter on the "Basics" 3.1.1, starting from page 40.

Figure 13: The figure shows the first Chiburi, described in Chapter 3.2.1, page 45. The form stems from the Eishin Ryu.

Figure 14: The figure shows the first Noto. It is described in Chapter 4.1.1 on page 49. Place the blunt backside of the blade on the scabbard.

Put the blade on the Saya with its backside

Lead the tip of the blade into the scabbard

Figure 15: Leading the tip of the blade into the Koiguchi of the Saya.

Figure 16: Push the scabbard over the blade until about two thirds of its length are covered.

Figure 17: Push the blade completely into the scabbard and then push both into the belt until only about two inches remain between your lower abdomen and the guard.

Figure 18: The right hand, holding the handle, slides slowly to its end and secures the sword by pushing it into the scabbard. Now the Habaki clips in the Koiguchi and the blade is safe. First align the sword in the belt and then pull the left foot to the right.

Figure 19: To finish the form stand up straight from the knees. Standing in a completely natural and relaxed posture you are ready to perform the next sword form.

Push the scabbard over the blade until about two thirds of its length are covered

Resheathe the sword completely

Secure the sword

Finish the form in a relaxed position

The connection to Aikido: In the form Uke Nagashi, for the first time a special movement called Irimi appears. It is a half step to the side with a body turn about 45° towards the opponent. It is very important that you make only a half step, not a full step. A full step will bring you in a bad position. You will not be able to avoid the attack properly, especially when you do not know the kind of attack that is imminent. Turning towards the opponent with a half step is also important. Without it you cannot face the enemy and are not able to exploit his blind spot. Irimi allows you to do both, to avoid the attack and to exploit the blind spot in front of or behind the opponent. It even gives you the advantage of being able to hit him at your will.

The next important thing to know is how to catch the cut. The sword teaches you to use the blunt backside of the blade because it is much more resistant than the cutting edge. As you can read in the previous chapter, the backside of the blade corresponds to the radial side of the forearm, whereas the cutting edge corresponds to the ulnar side. A cut must not be caught with the edge, and therefore you should never use the ulnar side of your forearm to block an attack. Using the radial side, you can catch the attack, deflect it, and defeat him in an instant. This method of dealing with a strike is exclusive to Aikido. It makes a big difference to the techniques of the other martial arts.

3 Ushirogiri

Meaning of the form Ushirogiri: The form Ushirogiri means to cut backward and corresponds to Sotokomen No Kaitennage in Aikido.

The enemy attacks with Shomen Uchi from behind. You make a half step to the right and leave the line of attack. Then you turn left and 180° to your rear, draw the sword and cut the opponent on his right side. Because he can step back you follow him immediately and finish him with a diagonal downward cut from his left shoulder to his right hip.

Pivot 180° to your left and cut the attacker on his right side

Finishing with Kaesagiri

Waiting for the opponent in a natural on guard stance

Make a first step left while releasing the sword catch

PERFORMING THE USHIROGIRI FORM

Figure 3: Stay in an upright position, feet together and the knees slightly bent. The heels touch each other and are lifted a little from the ground. Your weight should be evenly distributed on both feet. The arms are completely relaxed hanging on the sides of the body. You should neither fix your gaze on the opponent nor look downward.

Figure 4: Start with a step forward to the left. Note not to lift the toes while stepping but slide the foot instead. When you shift your weight onto your left foot, lift the heel of the right foot a little. Always keep the body upright and relaxed. Your left hand releases the sword's safety catch. Your right hand is laid on the handle from below with the side of the thumb. Make sure not to spread the thumb because the handle is there to protect the hand, wrist and fingers. With the step forward you should push the sword a little towards the opponent.

Make a second step with the right foot
with Irimi

Turn 180° to your left

Figure 5: Now make a half step about a shoulder width to the right. Take care not to take too large a step. Your toes should be pointing inwards and your knees should be slightly bent. The left heel must be lifted a little to allow the inward turn of the right foot. The left hand turns the Saya about 45° counterclockwise to the outside. This enables the right hand to grasp the handle naturally. Up to this point the sword is completely sheathed.

Figure 6: This is the third step of the form. Pivot 180° to your left on the balls of your feet. After that stay beside the line of attack with an upright body and knees bent for balance. Simultaneously drawing the sword until its tip is still just inside the scabbard you face the opponent, who remains on the centerline on your right side.

Step back with the left foot while cutting the side of the opponent

Make a crossover step forward with the left foot onto the centerline

Figure 7: Performing a step to the left rear, draw the sword completely and cut the opponent on his right side. The power for the cut is created by snapping the left hip back. Now stand in a deep and stable Zenkutsu Tachi. Make sure you pull the scabbard back as far as possible to facilitate the drawing of the blade. Then cut until your blade reaches the line of attack on your right side.

Figure 8: Now make a crossover step forward with your left foot back onto to the line of attack. Simultaneously draw the Saya in front of your lower abdomen and lift the sword over your head as if thrusting it into the sky.

Figure 9: Without pausing, make a large step forward to the right into Zenkutsu Tachi while grasping the sword with both hands and performing Kaesagiri Oroshi. The cut is drawn from the left shoulder of the opponent to his right hip and stops parallel to the ground.

Start the Kaesagiri

The figure shows Kaesagiri in its middle phase

Figure 10: It is important to extend both arms while cutting to reach the maximum range. Make sure you accelerate the sword with your left hand only. The right hand must be used only to give direction to the sword.

Figure 11: In order to stop the blade without using force, draw it back with your left hand after the tip has reached its maximum range. Do not use your right hand for stopping your sword as this will blunt your cut. Find out the correct timing when to draw back your sword.

Finish of the Kaesagiri

Perform Seigan without moving your feet

Perform Chiburi, its style stems from Eishin Ryu

Figure 12: After the cut perform Seigan without moving your feet, described in Chapter 3.1.1 on page 40.

Figure 13: The figure shows the first Chiburi, comprehensively described in Chapter 3.2.1, on page 45. The form stems from the Eishin Ryu.

Figure 14: The figure shows the first Noto. It is described in Chapter 4.1.1 on page 49. Place the blunt backside of the blade on the scabbard.

Put the sword on the Saya with its backside

Push the scabbard over the blade until about two thirds of its length are covered

Figure 15: Push the scabbard over the blade until about two thirds of its length are covered.

Figure 16: Push the blade completely into the scabbard and then push both into the belt until only about two inches remain between your lower abdomen and the guard.

Resheathe the sword completely

Slide the left foot to the right and
secure the sword

Finish the form
in a relaxed
position

Figure 17: The right hand, holding the handle, slides slowly to its end and secures the sword by pushing it into the scabbard. Now the Habaki clips in the Koiguchi and the blade is safe. First, align the sword in the belt and then pull the left foot to the right.

Figure 18: To finish the form you stand up straight from the knees. Standing in a completely natural and relaxed posture you are ready to perform the next sword form.

4 Zengogiri

Meaning of the form Zengogiri: Zengogiri means to cut forward and back. In Aikido, the form equals Ai Hanmi or Shomen Uchi No Shiho Nage.

In this scenario two aggressors are attacking from the front and back at the same time with the straight downward cut Shomen Uchi. After leaving the attack line to the right side, you cut the first aggressor with a Kiriage from his right hip to his left shoulder. Then you pivot 180° to your right and cut the attacker coming from behind with a Kaesagiri Oroshi from his left shoulder to his right hip.

The first aggressor is cut by Kiriage

The second attacker is cut by Kaesagiri Oroshi

Waiting for the opponent in a natural stance

Make the first step forward to the left while releasing the sword catch

PERFORMING THE ZENGOGIRI FORM

Figure 3: Stand in an upright position, feet together and the knees slightly bent. The heels touch each other and are lifted up a little from the ground. Your weight should be evenly distributed on both legs. The arms are completely relaxed hanging on the sides of the body. You should neither fix your gaze on the opponnent nor look downward.

Figure 4: Start with a step forward to the left. Note not to lift the toes while stepping but slide the foot. When you shift the weight onto the left foot, lift the heel of the right foot a little. Always keep the body upright and relaxed. The left hand releases the sword's safety catch. The right hand is laid on the handle from below with the side of the thumb. Make sure not to spread the thumb because the handle is there to protect the hand, wrist and fingers. With the step forward push the sword a little towards the opponent.

Make a second step to the right and perform Irimi

Close your feet

Figure 5: Now perform Irimi, stepping about a shoulder with to your right side beside the line of attack. Pivot on the balls of your feet about 45° towards your opponent with the toes pointing inwards. Do not draw the sword at this point yet.

Figure 6: Without pausing, close your feet, placing the left foot beside the right one. Bend your knees for balance while keeping your body upright. Simultaneously draw the sword until its tip is still just inside the scabbard, keeping the edge still upward. Therefore the cut of the opponent will not hit you and the blade will protect you against a horizontal cut. This will urge your opponent to step back in order to prepare for his next attack.

Perform a crossover step to the left
with Kiriage

Pivot 180° to your right when the cut
has reached its highest point

Figure 7: As the opponent strikes for a second time with a cut you leave the line of attack by making a left crossover step to your right. Simultaneously draw the blade completely, turning the edge up, and perform a Kiriage from the attacker's right hip to his left shoulder.

Figure 8: When the upward cut has reached its highest point, pivot under your sword 180° to your right.

Figure 9: Make a large step forward right into Zenkutsu Tachi and hit the second opponent coming from behind with a Kaesagiri Oroshi on his arms at the very moment he cuts downwards. It is very important to merge both cuts, the upward and the downward one, without any pause in between. To be able to do this in the correct manner, it is necessary that you perform both cuts only with the right hand.

Make a large step forward right with Kaesagiri Oroshi

Finish the Kaesagiri Oroshi parallel to the ground

Taking hold of the handle with the left hand too early while cutting downward will always cause a short break in the movement.

Figure 10: In order to stop the blade parallel to the ground, pull it back to your left hip only with the left hand.

Figure 11: Now perform Seigan, described in detail in Chapter 3.1.1, starting from page 40.

Perform Seigan without moving your feet

Perform Chiburi, its style stems from
Eishin Ryu

Place the blade on the scabbard

Figure 12: The figure shows the first Chiburi, completely described in Chapter 3.2.1, on page 45. The form stems from the Eishin Ryu.

Figure 13: The figure shows the first Noto. It is described in Chapter 4.1.1 on page 49. Place the blunt backside of the blade on the scabbard.

Figure 14: Push the scabbard over the blade until about two thirds of its length are covered.

Figure 15: Push the blade completely into the scabbard and then push both into the belt until only about two inches remain between your lower abdomen and the guard.

Figure 16: The right hand, holding the handle, slides slowly to its end and secures the sword by pushing it into the scabbard. Now the Habaki clips in the Koiguchi and the blade is safe. First, align the sword in the belt and then pull the left foot to the right.

Figure 17: To finish the form stand up straight from the knees. Standing in a completely natural and relaxed posture you are ready to perform the next sword form.

Push the scabbard over the blade until about two thirds of its length are covered

Resheathe the sword completely

Secure the sword

Finish the form in a relaxed position

The connection to Aikido: The basis for Shiho Nage is the body turn with two cuts to the front and back. Literally, Shiho Nage means "throw in four directions". Sometimes it is also called *sword throw* because you throw the partner as if cutting with a sword. The sword form clearly shows that the attacker's arm is brought, first of all diagonally upwards and outwards, and then back outwards and downwards. This is because you are performing a Kaesagiri and not a Shomen Uchi. Most people throw as if performing Shomen Uchi while training, since Ukemi is much easier and safer for the partner's shoulder. But it is wrong and not possible to perform in a real fight. There are many possibilities to block or counter a straight downward throw. The same thing can be said about the footwork. Many people step straight forward while pivoting 180° under the arm of Uke. But in the sword form you step to the side. This makes a big difference. When stepping to the side it is impossible to block or counter the throw because Uke is pulled to the side where he is off balance himself.

5 Sayugiri

Meaning of the form Sayugiri: The fourth form described in this book is Sayugiri, which means to cut first to the left and then to the right. In Aikido this form equates to Gyaku Hanmi No Shihonage.

In this form you fight against two aggressors attacking from your left and right. The first one is hit on his wrist while lifting his sword over his head and is then cut below his left arm. Then you pivot 180° to your left and swing your sword over your head. Without pausing you cut the second aggressor with Kaesagiri Oroshi from his left shoulder to his right hip.

The first aggressor is hit on his wrist

Then cut below his left arm

Pivot 180° to your left and swing the sword over your head

Finish with Kaesagiri Oroshi

Waiting for the opponent in a natural stance

Make the first step to the left, simultaneously releasing the sword catch

PERFORMING THE SAYUGIRI FORM

Figure 5: Stand in an upright position, feet together, knees slightly bent. The heels touch each other and are lifted up a little from the ground. Your weight should be evenly distributed on both legs. The arms are completely relaxed hanging on the sides of the body. You should neither fix your gaze on the opponent nor look downward.

Figure 6: Start with a step forward left. Note not to lift the toes while stepping but slide the foot. When you shift the weight onto the left foot, lift the heel of the right foot up a little. Always keep the body upright and relaxed. The left hand releases the sword's safety catch. The right hand is laid on the handle from below with the side of the thumb. Make sure not to spread the thumb because the handle is there to protect the hand, wrist and fingers. With the step forward push the sword a little towards the opponent.

Make a second step with the right foot and grasp the sword

Pivot to your right and draw the sword until its tip is still just sheathed

Figure 7: Turn the scabbard about 45° counterclockwise to the outside while making a step forward with the right foot. This enables the right hand to grasp the handle naturally.

Figure 8: Next you face the opponent on your right. Place your left foot in front of your right foot with the toes pointing to the right. Turn your hip and upper body to your right, bending your knees and lifting up the heel of your right foot. Simultaneously, draw your sword until only just the tip is still sheathed.

Cut to the opponent's right wrist   Perform a second cut below the armpit

Figure 9: Make a large step 90° to your right into Zenkutsu Tachi and draw your sword completely. Cut the opponent's right wrist, swinging the sword only in the right hand. Remember not to cut too deep because the enemy is holding the sword over his head.

Figure 10: After the wrist has been struck step back a little and to the right and cut the opponent below his left arm holding the sword only in your right hand. Turn the palm upward while cutting horizontally from the side. Take care to synchronize the cut with the step to create the momentum.

Pivot 180° to your left and cut the left attacker

Swing your sword over your head into Jodan No Kamae

Figure 11: After the attacker from the right was hit, pivot on the balls of your feet 180° to your left without pausing. Grasp the handle in both hands while turning. Close your feet and bend your knees for balance when you have finished the movement. Cut the attacker coming from the left side horizontally through his lower belly.

Figure 12: Do not try to stop the swing of the sword but lead it to the left and over your head until you will hold it in Jodan No Kamae. Take care to hold the sword at about 45°.

Start of the Kaesagiri Oroshi

Finish of the Kaesagiri Oroshi

Figure 13: Without pausing take a large step forward to the right into Zenkutsu Tachi and perform Kaesagiri Oroshi. The cut goes from the opponent's left shoulder to his right hip.

Figure 14: Finish the cut exactly parallel to the ground.

Figure 15: After finishing the cut let the sword sink very slowly into the Waki Gedan position. Hold the sword about two inches over your right knee with the cutting edge pointing diagonally upward. Take a minute for concentration, bring the blade to the center and lift it slowly until you change into Seigan.

Perform Waki Gedan No Kamae

Perform Seigan without moving your feet

Figure 16: Now perform Seigan, described in detail in Chapter 3.1.1., starting from page 40.

Figure 17: The figure shows the first Chiburi, described in Chapter 3.2.1, on page 45. The form stems from the Eishin Ryu.

Perform Chiburi, its style stems from Eishin Ryu

Place the backside of the blade on the scabbard

Push the scabbard over the blade until about two thirds of its length are covered

Figure 18: The figure shows the first Noto. It is described in Chapter 4.1.1 on page 49. Place the blunt backside of the blade on the scabbard.

Figure 19: Push the scabbard over the blade until about two thirds of its length are covered.

Figure 20: Completely push the blade into the scabbard and then push both into the belt until only about two inches remain between your lower abdomen and the guard.

Figure 21: The right hand, laid on the handle, slides slowly to its end and secures the sword by pushing it into the scabbard. Now the Habaki clips in the Koiguchi and the blade is safe. First align the sword in the belt and then pull the left foot to the right.

Resheathe the sword completely

Secure the sword

Figure 22: To finish stand upright from the knees. Standing in a completely natural and relaxed posture you are ready to perform the next sword form.

Finish the form in a relaxed position

The connection to Aikido: The connection between the sword form "Sayugiri" and Gyaku No Hanmi Shihonage becomes evident when imagining the transformation of the cut towards the Kote into the cut below the left armpit. With this movement, the arm of the attacker is prepared for being thrown when he is using a sword. It is essential to do the technique empty handed with a partner the same way as if doing it when using a sword, since otherwise the partner usually is not completely drawn off balance and will stand too stable for the technique to work properly. The point I wish to make here is that the technique cannot really be learned if Dori does not use a sword to get to practice it correctly. If the connection to sword combat is missing, Dori usually has no clue how to perform it in the correct way. The sword is the actual teacher. The technique cannot really be learned without it.

6 Tsuka Osae

Meaning of the form Tsuka Osae: The sixth form described in this book is Tsuka Osae, which means to grab hold of the handle of the defender's sword. In Aikido it equates to Gyaku Hanmi Katate Dori No Nikyo.

The attacker grabs hold of the handle of the defender's sword with his left hand in order to prevent the latter from drawing it and draws his own short sword with his right hand. The defender secures his sword in his right hand, steps to the right and thrusts it at the attacker's ribs with the end of the hilt. After that he turns the sword counterclockwise 180° over the attacker's left wrist, the edge facing downward, and performs Nikyo. This forces the attacker onto his knees and to let go of the handle. The defender draws his sword and forces the cowering attacker back, follows him and finishes him with a cut to the neck.

Thrust with the end of the handle

Performing Nikyo

The attacker is forced onto his knees

The cowering attacker is forced back by the blade

Finish the attacker with a cut to the neck

Controlling the enemy on the ground

PERFORMING THE TSUKA OSAE FORM

Figure 7: Stand in an upright position, feet together, the knees slightly bent. The heels touch each other and are lifted up a little from the ground. Your weight should be evenly distributed on both legs. The arms are completely relaxed hanging on the side of the body. You should neither fix your gaze on the opponent nor look downward.

Figure 8: While stepping forward with your left foot, the opponent grasps the handle near the guard. Immediately secure the sword by grasping the hilt with the right hand from below. Do not cover the Fuchi so that the thrust will have the greatest effect possible.

Figure 9: Leave the line of attack with a step to the right and push the end of the handle with force into the ribs on the left side of the opponent.

Waiting for the opponent in a natural position

With the first step with the left foot you secure the handle

Perform a Tsuki to the ribs

The figure shows Nikyo at the beginning

The figure shows Nikyo when finished

Figure 10: Draw your right foot back to the left one and turn 90° to the right without pausing and perform a deep and stable Kibadachi. Make sure to keep your body upright. Perform Nikyo by turning the sword counterclockwise 180° from the outside to the left and over the enemy's wrist, using the left hand. Then put pressure on the handle with your right hand.

Figure 11: The power of the leverage forces the opponent to let go of the Tsuka. Then draw your sword by pulling the scabbard from the blade. The blade will slide out of the sheath on its blunt backside. Note that drawing the blade may cause damage by cutting the scabbard and along with it your fingers as well. Therefore never draw a real sword out of the Saya with the edge facing downward but pull the Saya back.

Draw the sword and force the opponent back

Make a crossover step with the left foot and lift your sword as if thrusting it into the sky

Figure 12: Do not extend your legs while drawing the sword because the opponent cowers on the ground. Force him back with your blade. Therefore you have to snap your left hip back to create a momentum and keep your body stable. You should stand on the balls of your feet, not flat on the floor, in order to avoid leaning forward. In this posture it is necessary to press the heels together, bend the knees well and push them outward. Strong legs are needed to perform this position.

Figure 13: Because the opponent moves back you have to follow him with a crossover step with the left foot. Keep your hips deep while stepping forward. Do not turn the toes of your left foot outward. Use your left hand to pull the Saya in front of your lower abdomen. The right hand lifts the sword over the head as if thrusting it into the sky. Grasp the Tsuka with both hands. Moving, pulling the scabbard and lifting the sword should be done simultaneously.

Finish with Kaesagiri Oroshi

Perform Seigan without moving your feet

Figure 14: Next make a large right step forward into a deep Zenkutsu Tachi while cutting diagonally to the backside of the enemy's neck. Cut downward from the right to the left trying not to extend the legs, keeping the hips deep. The blade stops parallel to the ground with the handle about two inches in front of your left hip.

Figure 15: Now perform Seigan, described in detail in Chapter 3.1.1., starting from page 40.

Figure 16: The figure shows the first Chiburi, described in Chapter 3.2.1, on page 45. The form stems from the Eishin Ryu.

Perform Chiburi, its style stems from Eishin Ryu

Place the backside of the blade on the Saya

Figure 17: The figure shows the first Noto. It is completely described in Chapter 4.1.1 on page 49. Place the blunt backside of the blade on the scabbard.

Figure 18: Push the scabbard over the blade until about two thirds of its length are covered.

Push the scabbard over the blade until about two thirds of its length are covered

Resheathe the sword completely

Secure the sword

Finish the
form in a
relaxed
position

Figure 19: Push the blade completely into the scabbard and then push both into the belt until only about two inches remain between your lower abdomen and the guard.

Figure 20: The right hand, laid on the handle, slides slowly to its end and secures the sword by pushing it into the scabbard. Now the Habaki clips in the Koiguchi and the blade is safe. First you align the sword in the belt and then pull the left foot to the right.

Figure 21: To finish the form stand upright from the knees. Standing in a completely natural and relaxed posture you are ready to perform the next sword form.

7 Tekubi Osae

Meaning of the form Tekubi Osae: Tekubi Osae means to grasp hold of the wrist. In Aikido it equates to Ai Hanmi No Nikyo.

In this form the attacker grasps your right wrist in order to prevent you from drawing your sword. Step to your left while thrusting to his liver with the Fuchi. Then turn the handle clockwise from the left to the right and over the wrist of the attacker. This causes Nikyo which means twisting the wrist, thumb pointing downward. The technique forces the attacker down and to let go of your wrist. After that you turn 180° with Tai Sabaki and perform a horizontal cut to the rear of the enemy's neck. Finish by controlling the fallen opponent with your sword.

The enemy grasps your right wrist to prevent you from drawing your sword

Thrust with the Fuchi to his liver

Turn the handle clockwise over the attacker's wrist for Nikyo

Put pressure on the handle with your body weight and perform Nikyo

Draw your sword, at the same time pivot on your right foot

Cut horizontally to the rear of the neck by performing Tai Sabaki

Control the fallen opponent with your sword

Waiting for the opponent in a natural stance

With the first step left you unsecure the sword

PERFORMING THE TEKUBI OSAE FORM

Figure 8: Stand in an upright position, feet together, the knees slightly bent. The heels touch each other and are lifted up a little from the ground. Your weight should be evenly distributed on both legs. The arms are completely relaxed hanging on the sides of the body. You should neither fix your gaze on the enemy nor look downward.

Figure 9: You start with a step forward left. Note not to lift the toes while stepping but slide the foot. When you shift your weight onto the left foot, lift the heel of the right foot a little. Always keep your body upright and relaxed. The left hand releases the sword's safety catch. The right hand is laid on the handle from below with the side of the thumb. Make sure not to spread the thumb because the handle is there to protect the hand, wrist and fingers. With the step forward you should push the sword a little towards the opponent.

With a second step right you grasp the handle

Thrust to the liver with both hands performing a deep horse riding stance (Kibadachi in Japanese)

Figure 10: Make a step forward with the right leg. Turn the sword with your left hand about 45° counterclockwise to the outside. This enables the right hand to grasp the handle naturally when turning it over. At this moment the opponent attacks by grasping your right wrist to stop you drawing your sword.

Figure 11: Step to the left about 45° and perform a deep and stable Kibadachi. Thrust to the attacker's liver with the Fuchi, pushing the handle with both hands. Make sure to keep the sword in the center of your belly for maximum force.

Turn the handle clockwise over the enemy's wrist for Nikyo

Put pressure on the handle with your body weight and perform Nikyo

Figure 12: Without pausing you shift your weight onto the left leg and pull the right foot to your left. Simultaneously you swing the handle in a big circle clockwise from the left to the right and over the wrist of the attacker.

Figure 13: To perform Nikyo you put tremendous pressure on the handle with your body weight while sinking into a deep horse riding stance about 90° to your opponent. Turn the Mine to the outside. To avoid a very painful lever the opponent is forced to let go of the handle and fall down onto his knees.

Draw your sword to the left, pivoting on your right foot

Make a step forward with the left leg and start cutting the opponent's neck

Figure 14: Now pivot on your right foot and pull your left foot back in a circular motion, turning your left hip back as far as possible. Make sure to draw the scabbard away from the blade without moving it, not the blade out of the scabbard. Hold the sword in a 90° angle in front of your solar plexus with the cutting edge facing upward. Support the blade with your left index finger near its tip.

Figure 15: Next, make a step forward with the left foot, the toes turned inside, and start pivoting to your right while holding the blade horizontally about the level of your navel. Support the backside of the blade just behind the tip. The cutting edge is pointing towards the opponent's neck.

Figure 16: Pivot on your left foot and turn your body 180° to your right. This movement is called Tenkan Ashi. While turning, push the blade on its back near its middle section with your left hand, sliding towards the opponent's neck. Let the sword sink to about the level of your belt when you have finished the body turn.

Turn 180°, pivoting on your left foot and swing your right foot back while cutting

Step back with your left foot, close your feet and lift your sword into Jodan No Kamae

Figure 17: Close your feet by stepping back with your left foot and lift your sword very slowly over your head.

Figure 18: Make a large step back with your left foot and sink into a deep right forward stance while moving your sword in a huge circular motion very slowly until you perform Seigan.

Figure 19: The figure shows the first Chiburi, described in Chapter 3.2.1, on page 45. The form stems from the Eishin Ryu.

Make a large step back with your left foot and perform Seigan

Perform Chiburi, its style stems from Eishin Ryu

Put the backside of the blade on the scabbard

Figure 20: The figure shows the first Noto. It is described in Chapter 4.1.1 on page 49. Place the blunt backside of the blade on the scabbard.

Figure 21: Push the scabbard over the blade until about two thirds of its length are covered.

Figure 22: Push the blade completely into the scabbard and then push both into the belt until only about two inches remain between your lower abdomen and the guard.

Figure 23: The right hand, laid on the handle, slides slowly to its end and secures the sword by pushing it into the scabbard. Now the Habaki clips in the Koiguchi and the blade is safe. First align the sword in the belt and then pull the left foot to the right.

Figure 24: To finish the form stand upright from the knees. Standing in a completely natural and relaxed posture you are ready to perform the next sword form.

Push the scabbard over the blade until about two thirds of its length are covered

Resheathe the sword completely

Finish the form in a natural and relaxed posture

Secure the sword

8   Kawashi Tsuki

Meaning of the form Kawashi Tsuki: The form Kawashi Tsuki describes a twisting thrust to the heart and equates to Shomen Uchi No Sankyo Ura in Aikido.

The opponent attacks with a straight forward thrust. You make a half step to your left and pivot on your left foot to your right until your shoulders are parallel to the line of attack. At the same time you draw your sword. When your opponent lifts his sword again in order to strike you, hit him with a thrust to his heart. Before he falls in front of you, you finish him with a Kaesagiri Oroshi diagonal downward cut.

When the opponent attacks, step to the left while drawing your sword

Stepping back to the line and stab him in his heart

Step back again to the left and pull your sword out of the the now 'dead' body

Perform Kaesagiri Oroshi to the left before the opponent falls down

Waiting for the opponent in a natural stance

With the first step left release the catch of the sword

PERFORMING THE KAWASHI TSUKI FORM

Figure 5: Stand in an upright position, feet together, the knees slightly bent. The heels touch each other and are lifted up a little from the ground. Your weight should be evenly distributed on both legs. The arms are completely relaxed hanging on the sides of the body. You should neither fix your gaze on the opponent nor look downward.

Figure 6: First, step forward with the left leg. The left hand releases the sword catch while the right hand is laid on the handle from below with its radial side. This protects the right hand from being cut by the opponent.

Take a second step with the right foot and grasp the handle

Take a half step to the left performing Irimi

Figure 7: The second step is done with the right foot forward, turning the sword about 45° to the outside using the left hand. Therefore, the right hand is able to grasp the handle naturally from the side.

Figure 8: When the opponent attacks with a straight forwards, thrust, take a half step to the left, turn your body to your right and start drawing your sword.

Figure 9: Pivoting on your left foot, turn your body to your right until your shoulders are parallel to the line of attack. Close your feet and draw your sword completely. Hold it at about the level of your own heart, pointing towards the opponent with the backside facing you. Draw it back as far as possible. With your left hand hold the Saya at a 90° angle to your hips.

Figure 10: Next take a step back with the right foot onto the center line, your toes pointing towards the opponent. Bend your knees a little and lift the heel of your left foot for balance.

Pivot on your left foot turning right and draw your sword

Step back onto the centerline with the right leg and start the twisting thrust

At the same time pull the Saya with the left hand in front of your lower abdomen.

Figure 11: Pivot on your right foot and pull your left foot to the right. With a sharp turn of your hips to the left, thrust towards your opponent's heart, twisting the right hand clockwise until the blade is horizontal. Make sure to keep your shoulders parallel to the line of attack and to press the handle strongly against your forearm. Thrust at the level of your own heart to ensure you will hit your opponent's.

Pivot on your right foot to the left and finish the stabbing

Pull the sword out of the body while stepping forward with your left foot

Face your opponent, feet closed and lift your sword into Jodan No Kamae

Figure 12: With the next step you cross the center line again with your left foot, toes pointing towards the opponent. Bend your knees for balance and lift the heel of your right foot. Pull the sword back to your forehead with both hands, still holding the blade parallel to the ground. Note not to turn the sword upward with the edge, because in a real situation the blade would get stuck between two ribs.

Figure 13: Now close your feet by pulling the right one to the left and face your opponent. Lift the sword into Jodan No Kamae.

Figure 14: After a short pause perform Kaesagiri Oroshi from the opponent's right shoulder to his left hip. The force comes by stepping back with the right foot and letting the weight of your body sink down.

Step back with the right foot while cutting diagonally downward

Finish the cut in front of your right hip with the blade parallel to the floor

Figure 15: The cut stops horizontally with the handle about two inches in front of your right hip. Make sure that cutting and stepping back take place at the same time while keeping your body upright.

Figure 16: Now perform Seigan, described in detail in Chapter 3.1.1, starting from page 40.

Make a large step back with your left foot and perform Seigan

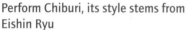

Perform Chiburi, its style stems from Eishin Ryu

Place the backside of the blade on the scabbard

Figure 17: The figure shows the first Chiburi, described in Chapter 3.2.1, on page 45. The form stems from the Eishin Ryu.

Figure 18: The figure shows the first Noto. It is described in Chapter 4.1.1 on page 49. Place the blunt backside of the blade on the scabbard.

Figure 19: You should lead the tip of the blade into the mouth of the scabbard without touching the steel.

Figure 20: Push the scabbard over the blade until about two thirds of its length are covered.

Lead the tip carefully into the mouth of the scabbard

Push the scabbard over the blade until about two thirds of its length are covered

Figure 21: Push the blade completely into the scabbard and then push both into the belt until only about two inches remain between your lower abdomen and the guard.

Resheathe your sword completely

Finish the form in a natural and relaxed posture

Secure your sword

Figure 22: The right hand, laid on the handle, slides slowly to its end and secures the sword by pushing it into the scabbard. Now the Habaki clips in the Koiguchi and the blade is safe. First align the sword in the belt and then pull the left foot to the right.

Figure 23: To finish the form stand upright from the knees. Standing in a completely natural and relaxed posture you are ready to perform the next sword form.

9 Tsukekomi

Meaning of the form Tsukekomi: Tsukekomi means to stick to the opponent and threaten him continously, giving him no chance to take the advantage back. In Aikido the form corresponds to Jodan Tsuki No Kote Gaeshi.

The opponent attacks with a forward thrust. You leave the line of attack with a half step to your right side, simultaneously turning towards the opponent, and deflect the thrust down your left side. When the opponent lifts his sword again, you hit him with Yokomen Uchi on his left forearm. Then you cross the line to the left side and perform a diagonal downward cut from your opponent's right shoulder to his left hip. Because he steps back and the cut misses him, you follow with a large step to the right thrusting towards his throat. You finish the form using the second Chiburi for the first time. This method stems from the Tenshin Shoden Katori Shinto Ryu.

Catch the thrust with the outside of your sword and deflect to the side

Cut with Yokomen Uchi to your opponent's left forearm

Perform Kaesagiri Oroshi from the left to the right

Stab towards your opponent's throat

Waiting for the opponent in a natural stance

Make a step forward with the left leg while releasing your sword catch

PERFORMING THE TSUKEKOMI FORM

Figure 5: Stand in an upright position, feet together and the knees slightly bent. The heels touch each other and are lifted up a little from the ground. Your weight should be evenly distributed on both legs. The arms are completely relaxed hanging on the sides of the body. You should neither fix your gaze on the opponent nor look downward.

Figure 6: Start by taking a step forward with the left foot. Note not to lift the toes while stepping but slide the foot. When you shift the weight onto your left foot, lift the heel of the right foot a little. Always keep your body upright and relaxed. The left hand releases the sword's safety catch. The right hand is laid on the handle from below with the side of the thumb. Make sure not to spread the thumb because the handle is there to protect the hand, wrist and fingers. With the step forward you should push the sword a little towards the opponent.

Make a second step to the right and grasp the sword while performing Irimi

Draw your sword and lead the thrust to your left side

Figure 7: The second step is called Irimi. It is a half step to the right side. Make sure not to turn the toes to the outside but towards your opponent. Simultaneously turn your hip to the left as far as possible.

Figure 8: You should try to keep your shoulders parallel to the line of attack in order to expose only a minimum of your body surface to your opponent's thrust. Draw the sword holding the scabbard vertically and lead the thrust to your left with the backside of the blade.

Swing your sword behind your head to the right rear

Perform Yokomen Uchi to your opponent's left forearm

Figure 9: Swing your sword around behind your head to the right rear without moving your feet.

Figure 10: At the very moment the Yokomen Uchi swings around your head and towards the opponent's forearm, shift your weight onto your right foot, pull the left foot to the right one and stand on the ball of the foot. Lean your body a little forward and extend your right arm as far as possible to reach the maximum range feasible. Stop the cut at the level of the head, while pulling the Saya in front of your lower abdomen with your left hand.

Figure 11: Next make a step forward with the left foot and perform a deep and stable Zenkutsu Tachi, shifting the weight of the body completely onto the left leg. Bend the left knee well and slide your right foot a little to your center. Lift the right heel up and face your opponent. Lift the sword over the head but avoid it tilting too far to the rear.

Make a large step forward with the left foot and perform Kaesagiri Oroshi

Start with the Kaesagiri Oroshi from the top of your head

Figure 12: Now perform a diagonal downward cut, called Kaesagiri Oroshi, from the right shoulder to your opponent's left hip.

Figure 13: Finish the cut exactly parallel to the ground by pulling the sword with the left hand to your right hip. This causes a momentum that stops the sword without you needing to use the right hand. Therefore the cut will not be blunted.

Finish the Kaesagiri Oroshi in front of your right hip

Shorten the distance for Tsuki with the right leg

Make a big step forward performing the Tsuki

Figure 14: Without pausing bring the sword to the center, performing Seigan by turning the hip to your left. Pull the right foot to the left and bend the knees for balance. Make sure to move the sword with your hip, not with your arms, which many people tend to do.

Figure 15: Make a large step forward with the right foot and thrust to the opponent's throat. The momentum comes from the hip movement. In order to reach the maximum range feasible extend the arms as far as possible. Hold the sword straight. Do not rotate the blade.

Figure 16: After you hit your opponent you must pull the sword out of the body and back in front of your lower abdomen. To neutralize the momentum it is necessary to pull your rear leg to the forward one simultaneously, closing your feet and bending your knees for balance.

Pull the sword out of the body

Make a step back for Seigan with the left foot

Figure 17: Now perform Seigan, described in detail in Chapter 3.1.1, starting from page 40.

Figure 18: Without moving your feet let your blade sink down very slowly until it stops exactly parallel to the ground. This posture is called Shira Seigan.

Figure 19: Next use the second form of Chiburi, described in Chapter 3.2.2 on page 45. This form stems from the Tenshin Shoden Katori Shinto Ryu.

Let the sword sink down slowly to Shira Seigan

Perform the second Chiburi, its style stems from the Katori Shinto Ryu

Place the sword on your left shoulder

Figure 20: The figure shows the second form of the Noto. Place the backside of the sword on your left shoulder. It is described in Chapter 4.1.2 on page 52.

Figure 21: Change the grip by grasping the handle with the right hand from below. The left hand grasps the Saya at the Koiguchi and pulls it forward. Place the blade on the scabbard at about its middle section with the backside of the sword.

Figure 22: Insert the tip of the blade into the Koiguchi and push the scabbard almost completely over the blade.

Figure 23: Now secure the sword by pushing it into the scabbard. At the same time slide your right foot back to the left and close your feet. The sword clips with the Habaki in the scabbard and will not fall out. First point the handle straight forward and then slide your left foot back to the right.

Figure 24: To finish the form stand upright from your knees. Standing in a completely natural and relaxed posture you are ready to perform the next sword form.

Change the grip on your handle and lead the tip into the scabbard

Push the scabbard over the blade until about two thirds of its length are covered

Secure the sword

Finish the form in a relaxed position

10 Tsume

Meaning of the form Tsume: The tenth form is Tsume, meaning to drive the opponent into a corner, corresponds to Irimi Nage in Aikido.

At the moment of attack you perform Irimi to the right, in combination with a cut to the Kote. The attacker steps back and raises his sword. You cross the line of attack from right to left with a deep Kibadachi. At the same time you cut with Kiriage from down below right to above left. You leave the line of attack completely, pivoting to the right and attack the opponent with Yokomen Uchi to the right hand side of his throat. Slide back into Shin No Kamae. The line of your shoulders should be at an angle of 45° to the line of attack. The retreating opponent is then threatened by a thrust to his throat.

The attacker retreats more and you follow and threaten him with Shomen Uchi to his forearm. After that you point towards his throat with the Kissaki and force him to submit.

Perform Irimi and cut to the Kote

Step left to Kibadachi and cut with Kiriage

Hit with Yokomen Uchi to the right hand side of the neck

Slide back into Shin No Kamae

Make a step forward with the left foot and and perform Jodan No Tsuki

Follow the retreating opponent with a sliding step and perform Shomen Uchi

Force the attacker to submit by pointing towards his throat

Waiting for the opponent in a natural stance

With the first step left release your sword catch

PERFORMING THE TSUME FORM

Figure 8: Stand in an upright position, feet together, the knees slightly bent. The heels touch each other and are lifted up a little from the ground. Your weight should be evenly distributed on both legs. The arms are completely relaxed hanging on the sides of the body. You should neither fix your gaze on the opponent nor look downward.

Figure 9: Start with a step forward with the left foot. Note not to lift the toes while stepping but slide the foot. When you shift the weight onto your left foot, lift the heel of the right one a little. Always keep the body upright and relaxed. The left hand releases the sword's safety catch. The right hand is laid on the handle from below with the side of the thumb. Make sure not to spread the thumb because the handle is there to protect the hand, wrist and fingers. With the step forward you should push the sword a little towards the opponent.

Make a second step to the right with Irimi

Cut to the attacker's Kote

Figure 10: The figure shows the outside Irimi. It is completely described in Chapter 2.2 on page 26. Make a half step forward to the right, the toes pointing in an inward direction. The hips and the upper body turn about 45° to the left in order to avoid getting hit. Make sure not to lean forward. The Tsuka points towards your opponent. Twist it counterclockwise to the outside, while the right hand grasps the handle from below.

Figure 11: Place your left foot just behind the right one with slightly bent knees. At the same time draw your sword and cut diagonally to your opponent's left wrist.

Step left to Kibadachi and perform Kiriage

Pivot to the right with Yokomen Uchi

Figure 12: Without pausing cross the line of attack with a deep Kibadachi, turn the edge upward and cut from your opponent's left hip to his right shoulder.

Figure 13: Next, cut to the right side of the attacker's throat. Pivot on your left foot to the right and pull your right foot to the left one.

Figure 14: Without pausing slide your right foot backwards in a 45° angle to the line of attack and into the Shin No Kamae position. Simultaneously draw the sword along your opponent's neck and twist the edge upward at the end of the motion. Make sure that the tip of the blade threatens the attacker's heart.

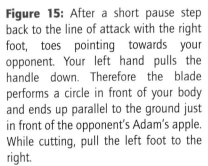

Step right back into Shin No Kamae

Force the opponent back with Kiriage

Figure 15: After a short pause step back to the line of attack with the right foot, toes pointing towards your opponent. Your left hand pulls the handle down. Therefore the blade performs a circle in front of your body and ends up parallel to the ground just in front of the opponent's Adam's apple. While cutting, pull the left foot to the right.

Figure 16: Your right hand grasps the Tsuka from below and your left hand from above. Keep the elbows down. From this position you are able to stab towards your opponent's throat immediately.

Threaten the opponent with Jodan No Tsuki, feet together

Swing the sword to the right while making a step forward with the right foot

Make a sliding step to the right with Shomen Uchi

Figure 17: The opponent retreats and you follow him with large step with the right foot. Simultaneously let the tip of your sword fall to the right and use the momentum to lift it to Jodan No Kamae.

Figure 18: Pull the left foot to your right. Simultaneously threaten your opponent's forearm in Jodan No Kamae with Shomen Uchi. Keep your body upright and both knees slightly bent.

Figure 19: Step back with the left foot to Zenkutsu Tachi, while threatening your opponent's Adam's apple with the tip of your blade. This is called Seigan.

Figure 20: Without changing your position, let the blade sink down slowly until it is horizontal to the ground. This stance is called Shira Seigan.

Step back with the left foot into Seigan

Let the sword sink down to Shira Seigan

Figure 21: Next use the second form of Chiburi, described in Chapter 3.2.2 on page 45. This form stems from the Tenshin Shoden Katori Shinto Ryu.

Perform Chiburi, its style stems from Katori Shinto Ryu

Place the sword on your left shoulder   Lead the Kissaki into the Koiguchi

Figure 22: The figure shows the second form of the Noto. Place the backside of the sword on your shoulder. It is described in Chapter 4.1.2 on page 52.

Figure 23: Change the grip by grasping the handle with the right hand from below. The left hand grasps the Saya at the Koiguchi and pulls it forward. Place the blade on the scabbard about its middle section with the backside of the sword.

Figure 24: Lead the tip of the blade in the Koiguchi and push the scabbard almost completely over the blade.

Figure 25: You must secure the sword by pushing it into the scabbard. At the same time slide back with your right foot to the left and close your feet. The sword clips with the Habaki in the scabbard and will not fall out. First align the sword in the belt and then slide your left foot back to the right.

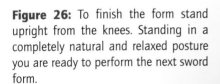

Push the scabbard over the blade until about two thirds of its length are covered

Resheathe the sword completely and secure it

Figure 26: To finish the form stand upright from the knees. Standing in a completely natural and relaxed posture you are ready to perform the next sword form.

Finish the form in a relaxed position

11 Sanpo

Meaning of the form Sanpo: The eleventh form of this curriculum is Sanpo which means cutting in three directions. In Aikido it equates to Shomen Uchi No Uchi Kaiten Sankyo.

You are threatened by three adversaries around you. They attack from the front, from the left and from the right. However, not all at once since they might easily wound each other. You catch the first cut and wound the aggressor on his wrist with Shomen Uchi. Then you turn to your right and perform Kiriage from the right hip to the left shoulder of your second opponent. After that you pivot 180° and cut the last one with a Do Uchi from left to right through the abdomen and finish him with a Kaesagiri Oroshi from his right shoulder to his left hip.

Catch the first cut with the Mine

Wound your second adversary's forearm with Shomen Uchi

Cut your second opponent with Kiriage from the left to the right

Wound your third aggressor with Do Uchi from left to right

After the Do Uchi a Kaesagiri Oroshi from right to left is performed

Turn the Mine to the outside when drawing the sword

Waiting for the opponent in a natural stance

Make a step forward with the left foot while releasing the sword catch

PERFORMING THE SANPO FORM

Figure 7: Stand in an upright position, feet together, the knees slightly bent. The heels touch each other and are lifted up a little from the ground. Your weight should be evenly distributed on both legs. The arms are completely relaxed hanging on the sides of the body. You should neither fix your gaze on the opponent nor look downward.

Figure 8: First make a step forward with the left foot and turn the Mine of the sword clockwise to the outside with your left hand (as shown in detail in Figure 6).

Figure 9: Without pausing you close your feet, sliding the right foot to the left one. Grasp the handle the very moment your feet are closed. Do not put your right foot flat on the floor but slide it about shoulder width to your right. This is a feint to provoke your opponent's attack.

Close your feet, sliding the right foot to the left

Make a step to your right while catching the opponent's cut

Figure 10: Slide to the right and draw your sword over your head. Turn the Mine outward to protect yourself.

Figure 11: Pull the left foot to the right. Bend your knees for balance. Grasp the sword with both hands and lift it over the center of your head. This is called Jodan No Kamae.

Lift your sword to Jodan No Kamae

Wound the opponent's wrist with
Shomen Uchi while stepping back with
the left foot

Prepare the Kiriage by turning
the cutting edge towards the opponent

Figure 12: Step back with your left foot while performing Shomen Uchi to the opponent's wrist.

Figure 13: Next perform Kiriage to your right. First it is necessary to turn the cutting edge towards the opponent. Turn the sword with the left hand while the right hand grasps the handle from above. It is very important to turn the edge before cutting.

Figure 14: Your second attacker is cut with Kiriage from his right hip to his left shoulder. Make sure to use the force of your hips for cutting, and not the strength of your arms. The force of the hips is created by shifting your body weight from your left leg to the right in the same plane. Therefore you should not stretch your legs while turning your hips. Now the movement will be described step by step. First step

Perform the Kiriage in a deep Kibadachi

Finish the Kiriage

back with the right foot into a forward leaning stance, left foot forward. Then turn your hip sharply to your right and perform a deep horse riding stance. In this position cut diagonally upward from the left to the right. Make sure to keep your back straight while cutting.

Figure 15: When the cut reaches its highest point turn your hips until you perform a forward leaning stance with the right foot just 180° in the opposite direction.

Swing the sword to your left and over your head

Place the sword on your left elbow

Figure 16: Using the momentum of the sword, pull the left foot to the right and keep on turning 270°. Finish with your feet closed and knees slightly bent for balance. Swing the sword in a circular motion over your head and to your left until it is placed with the backside of the blade on your left elbow.

Figure 17: While the Mine is lying on your left elbow align the blade horizontally. Now make a large step to your right, performing a deep and stable horse riding stance (Kibadachi in Japanese).

Figure 18: Cut horizontally through your enemy's lower belly. Stop the blade on your right side.

Figure 19: Pull the left foot to the right. Let the tip of the blade fall down to your left and use the momentum to lift the sword into Jodan No Kamae. Make sure to keep your elbows deep.

Cut through your third opponent's lower abdomen with a Do Uchi

Swing the sword to your left side and over your head

Figure 20: After a short pause perform a Kaesagiri Oroshi from your opponent's left shoulder to his right hip. Remember to extend your arms as far as feasible when cutting to reach the maximum range possible. Make a step back with the left foot while cutting.

Finish the third opponent with Kaesagiri Oroshi

Finish of the Kaesagiri Oroshi

Hold the sword over your right knee with the cutting edge to the front

Figure 21: Finish the Kaesagiri Oroshi parallel to the ground by pulling the sword back with your left hand.

Figure 22: After finishing the cut, hold the sword over your right knee in Waki Gedan No Kamae. Because the cutting edge is pointing forward you are able to counter any attack with a powerful Kiriage.

Figure 23: After a short pause for concentration, align the sword on the center line performing Gedan No Kamae. Then lift your Katana very slowly for Seigan.

Figure 24: One of the most important positions is called Seigan. The basis of it is Zenkutsu Tachi, described here as the forward stance leading with the right leg. When doing Zenkutsu Tachi the right knee is bent at an angle of almost 90° and you stand deep and wide. The right knee and the right foot point inwards. Your weight rests almost completely on your front leg. The left leg is almost straight. The left heel is lifted up a little from the ground. The toes point in a forward direction.

Align the sword on the center line

Lift the point of the blade for Seigan

The head, back and the leg form a straight line. This is a very stable position in which as little of your body's silhouette as possible is exposed to the aggressor. It is important to have the left leg stretched out as otherwise the position would be quite weakened. The body is upright, shoulders and arms are completely relaxed. The hip is closed firmly and not opened. The lower body and the legs are tensed. Dori's concentration is focused on his Hara, a point below the navel about the width of a hand.

The sword has to be held with the handle about two inches in front of the lower belly. The hands are slightly turned inward while holding the handle not too firm. The Kissaki points towards the opponent's left eye, protecting the right wrist. You should observe all around, not fixing your gaze on anything in particular. Adopt an inner posture which enables the brain to notice any movement that is about to occur in order be able to react instantly should any sign of life be left in your opponent or should another aggressor come near you. The position of the sword and the posture of the body along with the attitude will work together and help perform Seigan, called the posture of the clear eyes.

Let the sword sink down slowly to Shira Seigan

Perform Chiburi, its style stems from the Katori Shinto Ryu

Figure 25: Then let the sword sink down again until it is exactly parallel to the ground without moving your feet. This position is called Shira Seigan. It is used to prepare the second form of Chiburi.

Figure 26: Next use the second form of Chiburi, completely described in Chapter 3.2.2 on page 45. This form stems from the Tenshin Shoden Katori Shinto Ryu.

Figure 27: The figure shows the second form of the Noto. Place the backside of the sword on your shoulder. It is described in Chapter 4.1.2 on page 52.

Place the backside of the blade on your left shoulder

Lead the tip of the blade into the Koiguchi

Figure 28: Change the grip by grasping the handle with the right hand from below. The left hand grasps the Saya at the Koiguchi and pulls it forward. Place it on the scabbard with the backside of the sword about the middle section of the blade.

Figure 29: Insert the tip of the blade into the Koiguchi and push the scabbard almost completely over the blade.

Push the scabbard over the blade until about two thirds of its length are covered

30

Secure the sword

31

Finish the form in a relaxed position

Figure 30: You must secure the sword by pushing it into the scabbard. At the same time slide back your right foot to the left one and close your feet. The sword clips with the Habaki in the scabbard and will not fall out. First move the handle exactly parallel to where you are looking, then you slide your left foot back to the right one.

Figure 31: To finish the form stand upright from the knees. Standing in a completely natural and relaxed posture you are ready to perform the next sword form.

12 Shiho

Meaning of the form Shiho: Shiho means four directions. The sword form equates to Shomen Uchi No Shiho Nage in Aikido.

There are four aggressors attacking you from four different directions at the same time. You avoid the first cut by stepping to the right and strike your opponent, who is now retreating with a powerful Shomen Uchi. Then you turn to your right and perform Kiriage from the left to the right. Without stopping the flowing motion of the Katana, you turn round and perform Kaesagiri Oroshi from the right to the left. After that you lead the sword to your left attacking the last opponent, the latter coming from behind, with a thrust to his throat. Because he also retreats, you follow with a large forward step and finish with the same powerful downward cut, which has already been applied to 'kill' the first opponent.

In this sword form you will use the third method of Chiburi for the first time. You will also learn how to let your sword flow from one attacker to the other without stopping. Therefore, performing Shiho will tremendously improve your skills in martial arts.

The first aggressor attacks with Shomen Uchi

Catch the attack with the backside of your blade

Cut the first opponent with a powerful
Shomen Uchi

Cut the second opponent with a
Kiriage from the left to the right

Cut the third opponent with Kaesagiri
Oroshi from the right to the left

Threaten the last opponent with a
thrust to his throat

Finish the last opponent with a
powerful Shomen Uchi

| Waiting for the opponent in a natural stance | Make a step forward with the left foot while releasing the sword catch |

PERFORMING THE SHIHO FORM

Figure 8: Stand in an upright position, feet together, the knees slightly bent. The heels touch each other and are lifted up a little from the ground. Your weight should be evenly distributed on both legs. The arms are completely relaxed hanging on the sides of the body. You should neither fix your gaze on the opponent nor look downward.

Figure 9: First make a step forward wih the left foot and turn the Mine of the sword clockwise to the outside with your left hand.

Close your feet by sliding the right foot to the left one

Make a step to your right while catching the cut of your opponent

Figure 10: Without pausing close your feet, sliding the right foot to the left. Grasp the handle the very moment your feet are closed. Do not put your right foot flat on the floor but slide it about shoulder width to your right. This is a feint to provoke an attack from your opponent.

Figure 11: Slide to the right and draw your sword over your head. Turn the Mine outward to protect yourself.

Figure 12: Place the left foot to the right. Bend your knees for balance. Grasp the sword with both hands and lift it over the center of your head. This is called Jodan No Kamae.

Lift your sword into Jodan No Kamae

Make a large step forward, close your feet and perform Shomen Uchi

Figure 13: Threatened by the downward cut, the opponent retreats. Follow with a large step forward with the right foot and perform a strong Shomen Uchi. Make sure you accelerate the sword only with the left hand and extend the arms as far as possible for the maximum range. The right hand must be turned over the handle to apply maximum pressure when you make contact with something. You should cut with the motion and almost as if you are of throwing your sword away. Support the cut by pushing your body weight forward with the impetus of your left leg.

Cut down sharply until the tip stops only one inch above the floor

Place the backside of the blade on your left shoulder preparing for Kiriage

Figure 14: The force of the cut creates a strong forward momentum. Therefore you need good skills to neutralize it in order to avoid losing your balance. To do so, pull your left leg to the right and stop with closed feet. Bend your knees and let your body weight sink down deeply. Make sure to keep your back straight. Cut down as far as about one inch above the ground where the tip of the blade should come to a halt.

Figure 15: Place the blade with the Mine on your left shoulder, the tip facing upward. Change the grip and grasp the Tsuka with your right hand on its lower side.

Perform Kiriage from a deep Kibadachi

The figure shows the end position of the Kiriage from the front

Figure 16: Now turn to your right in order to perform Kiriage. Pivot 90° on your left foot and step to your right into a deep horse riding stance. It is important to align the edge of the blade to the right before cutting.

Figure 17: Perform the Kiriage while stepping to your right into Kibadachi. Use the force of your body weight, shifting from your left to the right. Make sure you do not use the strength of your arms for cutting but move your body's center of gravity instead.

Swing your sword to the right, and using the momentum, turn 180° to the rear

Perform a Kaesagiri Oroshi from the right to the left

Figure 18: Use the momentum of the sword to pivot on your right foot 180° to the rear when the cut reaches its highest point. Close your feet and bend your knees for balance. Swing your sword in a circular motion over your head without stopping even for a split second.

Figure 19: Step back with your left foot diagonally to your left and perform a right leg leading forward stance while cutting diagonally downward from your third opponent's left shoulder to his right hip.

Figure 20: Without stopping the flowing motion of the sword, turn to your left. Let the blade swing from below to the level of your opponent's throat. Stop it there parallel to the ground with the edge in an upward position. Threaten him with a thrust holding the handle with your right hand and cover the Fuchi with your left hand just in case stabbing might be necessary. Keep your elbows deep and close your feet.

Let the sword flow to the left for Jodan Tsuki

Swing your sword to your right using its weight to lift it over your head

Figure 21: Without moving your feet, let the tip of the blade fall down to your right and use the momentum to lift the sword into Jodan No Kamae. Make sure to keep your elbows deep.

Figure 22: Because the enemy retreats, follow him with Shomen Uchi in the same manner as when cutting your first opponent.

Make a large step while performing Shomen Uchi

Cut down to the ground with closed feet

Step left back for Seigan

Figure 23: Finish the strong Shomen Uchi as you did when cutting your first opponent.

Figure 24: Step back with your left foot and perform Zenkutsu Tachi. Lift the sword slowly for Seigan, and then let it sink down into Gedan.

Figure 25: The figure shows Gedan No Kamae. Hold the blade naturally pointing towards the fallen opponent.

Figure 26: Now perform the third Chiburi, its style stems from the Suio Ryu. Pull the sword with the left hand towards your left shoulder, supporting the handle with the index finger of your right hand near the guard. Holding the sword diagonally in front of your navel you are able to thrust at the opponent lying in front of you at your will.

Let the sword sink down slowly into Gedan

Perform Chiburi, its style stems from Suio Ryu

Figure 27: Without changing the posture, grasp the handle with your right hand near the guard from above. Now remove your left hand from the Tsuka and grasp the sheath near the Koiguchi. Make sure not to move the Katana.

Grasp the scabbard preparing to resheathe the sword

Place the backside of the blade on the Saya

Push the Saya over the blade about two thirds of its length

Figure 28: Let the tip of the blade fall down and use the momentum to swing the sword upward until its backside touches the scabbard near the guard. Pull the Saya back as far as possible and lead the Kissaki carefully into the Koiguchi to avoid injury to your left hand.

Figure 29: Push the scabbard over the blade until about two thirds of its length are covered.

Figure 30: Push the blade completely into the scabbard and then push both into the belt until only about two inches remain between your lower abdomen and the guard.

Figure 31: The right hand is laid on the handle and slowly slides to its end and secures the sword by pushing it into the scabbard. Now the Habaki clips in the Koiguchi and the blade is safe. First align the sword in the belt and then pull the left foot to the right.

Resheathe the sword completely

Secure the sword

Figure 32: To finish the form stand upright from your knees. Standing in a completely natural and relaxed posture you are ready to perform the next sword form.

Finish the form in a relaxed position

13 Nukiawase

Meaning of the form Nukiawase: Nukiawase means to draw the sword and match the attack. The form corresponds to Yokomen Uchi No Gokyo in Aikido.

The opponent attacks before you are able to draw the sword. Therefore, you step back with your left foot and then draw the sword. After that you cut with Shomen Uchi to the attacker's forearm. Your opponent retreats and then returns again for a renewed strike. You follow him immediately and thrust with a Tsuki to his belly. The opponent retreats yet again while cutting. You leave the line of attack to the right and deliver a Yokomen Uchi. The opponent steps back for the third time. Now you finish him with Kaesagiri Oroshi from his right shoulder to the left hip. You step back and control the fallen opponent from a position, which allows you to stab him at your will.

The opponent attacks with Shomen Uchi

Try to cut the Kote

Force your opponent back with a stab to his belly

Follow your opponent with Yokomen Uchi

Finish the opponent with Kaesagiri Oroshi

Control the fallen opponent with your sword

Waiting for the opponent in a natural stance

Make a step forward with the left foot and provoke your opponent to attack you

PERFORMING THE NUKIAWASE FORM

Figure 7: Stand in an upright position, feet together, the knees slightly bent. The heels touch each other and are lifted up a little from the ground. Your weight should be evenly distributed on both legs. The arms are completely relaxed hanging on the sides of the body. You should neither fix your gaze on the opponent nor look downward.

Figure 8: Start with a step forward with the left foot. Note not to lift the toes while stepping but slide the foot. When you shift the weight onto the left foot, lift the heel of the right foot up a little. Always keep the body upright and relaxed. The left hand releases the sword's safety clip. The right hand is laid on the handle from below with the side of the thumb. Make sure not to spread the thumb because the handle is there to protect the hand, wrist and fingers. With the step forward you should push the sword a little towards the opponent.

Step left back, close your feet and draw your sword

Lift your sword into Jodan No Kamae

Figure 9: At the moment the opponent attacks, you move back closing your feet. Do not draw the blade out of the sheath, but pull the Saya back and away from the blade. To facilitate the process of drawing the sword without damaging the Saya you have to pull the scabbard back as far as possible.

Figure 10: The opponent's attack misses your forearm and you can draw the sword completely. Your feet are closed and the knees are slightly bent. Lift your sword over your head and grasp it with both hands.

Step back again with the left foot and perform Shomen Uchi

Stab your opponent's belly while stepping forward with the left foot

Figure 11: Step back with the left foot and perform Shomen Uchi in order to hit your opponent's wrist. Try to synchronize the step with the cut to neutralize the momentum of the sword. Finish with the blade parallel to the ground.

Figure 12: Without pausing make a step forward with the left foot, performing a Tsuki to your adversary's belly, thus forcing him back. The momentum should come from your legs and hips. Do not use the force of your arms for stabbing.

Figure 13: Follow with Irimi to the right. Make a half step to the right and pivot on your right foot some 45° to your left. Make sure the toes of your feet are turned towards the opponent. At the same time lift your sword over your head as if stabbing into the sky.

Step to the right with Irimi

Pivot on your right foot, close your feet and perform Yokomen Uchi

Figure 14: Without pausing follow with Yokomen Uchi to your opponent's left temple. To do this extend your arms for maximum range and stop the cut at the level of your own head. Use the body turn to the left for the momentum, together with pulling your left foot to the right.

Figure 15: Now make a large step forward, performing Zenkutsu Tachi. Lift your sword over your head preparing for Kaesagiri Oroshi. Make sure you hold it at a 45° angle.

Make a large step forward with the left leg and lift your sword into Jodan No Kamae

Perform a strong Kaesagiri Oroshi in a deep left leg leading forward stance with the left leg

Finish the Kaesagiri Oroshi parallel to the ground

Figure 16: Perform a strong Kaesagiri Oroshi from your opponent's right shoulder to his left hip, using the momentum of the forward step. The force comes from the acceleration of your body weight. Therefore you should synchronize the cut with the step. The cut should reach its maximum range the very moment the right foot touches the ground.

Figure 17: Finish the Kaesagiri Oroshi parallel to the ground in front of your right hip. Keep your upper body upright. Do not lean sideways while cutting. Pull the sword back with your left hand, using the momentum to stop the sword.

Figure 18: Step back with the left foot and perform Zenkutsu Tachi while lifting the Katana slowly to Seigan.

Figure 19: Keep this posture and let the sword sink down slowly into the Gedan position.

Lift the blade for Seigan

Let the sword slowly sink to Gedan No Kamae

Figure 20: The right hand grasps the handle from above with the thumb facing towards your own body. Turn the left hip back while doing it.

Grasp the handle in a Gyaku Te hold and twist the blade

Control the opponent with your sword

Perform Chiburi, its style stems from Suio Ryu

Figure 21: By lowering your right elbow twist the edge until it is pointing upwards. Place the left hand on the Fuchi. Hold the sword at a 45° angle pointing towards the fallen opponent and threaten him with a thrust.

Figure 22: To shake the blood from the blade, the back of your left hand is slapped against your right forearm from underneath.

Figure 23: The figure shows the Chiburi from a different angle. You can clearly see the angle of the blade and underneath.

Figure 24: Now place the left index finger on the back of the blade at about its middle section. Align the sword horizontally in front of your lower abdomen. Twist the right hand to the outside until the elbow is some 90° in front of your right hip. At the same time lift the blade with your index finger sliding on the Mine to about three inches before its tip. Hold the blade horizontally about three inches in front of your lower belly with the cutting edge facing forward.

Chiburi from a different angle

Put the Kissaki on the Koiguchi

Figure 25: Now the left hand grabs the Koiguchi. Put the backside of the blade on the scabbard. Support the Mine with your left thumb and index finger while leading the tip into the sheath. While resheathing the sword you should twist the blade and the scabbard simultaneously and continuously with the edge upward. Be careful while doing it with a real Katana in order to avoid injury.

Lead the tip of the blade into the mouth of the sheath

Push the scabbard over the blade until about two thirds of its length are covered

Resheathe the sword and secure it

Finish the form in a relaxed position

Figure 26: Lead the blade into the sheath for about three inches. Then push the scabbard over the blade until only the Habaki is still unsheathed.

Figure 27: Resheathe the sword completely while sliding back with your right foot and secure it by putting some pressure on the Fuchi. At the same time push it back into your belt. The guard stops about two inches in front of your lower belly the moment you close your feet.

Figure 28: To finish the form stand upright from your knees. Standing in a completely natural and relaxed posture you are ready to perform the next sword form.

14 Todome

Meaning of the form Todome: Todome means to stop the "enemy" while he is attacking and 'kill' him immediately. The form equates to Shomen Uchi No Yonkyo in Aikido.

The opponent attacks with Shomen Uchi. You step to the right with Irimi, draw your sword and perform Kiriage while making a crossover step with your left foot to the right. The cut is drawn from the opponent's right hip to his left shoulder. After cutting him you follow with a stab to his heart. 'Mortally wounded' your opponent falls forward. Therefore you step back with your right foot and kneel down a bit on your left knee. You finish your opponent with a thrust to his throat. Then you perform the first Chiburi.

Perform Kiriage while making a crossover step with the left leg

Step back with the left foot and perform a deep Kibadachi

Pull the left foot to the right and stab at your opponent's heart

Step back with your right foot and lift your sword into Jodan No Kamae

Kneel down on your left knee and stab at your opponent's neck

Control the enemy and be prepared to cut again if necessary

Hold your sword parallel to the ground to prepare for Chiburi

The figure shows the Bokken from a different angle

Waiting for the opponent in a natural stance

Make a step forward with the left foot while releasing the sword catch

PERFORMING THE TODOME FORM

Figure 9: Stand in an upright position, feet together, the knees slightly bent. The heels touch each other and are lifted up a little from the ground. Your weight should be evenly distributed on both legs. The arms are completely relaxed hanging on the sides of the body. You should neither fix your gaze on the opponent nor look downward.

Figure 10: Start with a step forward with the left foot. Note not to lift the toes up while stepping but slide the foot. When you shift your weight onto your left foot, lift the heel of the right foot a little. Always keep the body upright and relaxed. The left hand releases the sword's safety catch. The right hand is laid on the handle from below with the side of the thumb. Make sure not to spread the thumb because the handle is there to protect the hand, wrist and fingers. With the step forward you should push the sword a little towards the opponent.

Step to the right with Irimi and grasp the sword

Make a crossover step left and perform Kiriage

Figure 11: The figure shows the outside Irimi, as described in Chapter 2.2 on page 26. Make a half step forward to the right, the toes pointing inward. The hips and the upper body turn about 45° to the left in order to avoid getting hit. Make sure not to lean forward.

Figure 12: Without pausing you make a crossover step with the left leg to Kake Tachi in front of your right foot. The left foot is turned with the toes some 90° outwards standing flat on the floor. The rear leg is also bent and the knee pushes into the calf of the forward leg for balance while lifting the heel up a little. At the same time you draw the sword by twisting the cutting edge down and perform Kiriage from the right hip of your opponent to his left shoulder. Make sure to pull back the sheath as far as possible to avoid injury.

Step back with your left foot for Kibadachi

Pull the left foot to the right while stabbing at your opponent's heart

Figure 13: When the Kiriage has reached its highest point, draw the sword back in front of your solar plexus with both hands. Holding the blade horizontally with the cutting edge to the outside, point towards your opponent's heart and step back with the left foot performing a deep horse riding stance parallel to the line of attack.

Figure 14: Without pausing pull the left foot to the right and stab at your opponent's heart, still holding the blade horizontally.

Step back with the right foot and pull the sword up to the forehead

Slide back the left foot to the right and lift your sword into Jodan No Kamae

Figure 15: Now you step back with the right foot while pulling the sword with both hands up to your forehead. Do not twist the blade while pulling. Make sure that there is a 90° angle between you and your sword.

Figure 16: Because the 'wounded' opponent falls in front of you, it is necessary to step back with your left foot, then close your feet and lift your Katana into Jodan No Kamae.

Figure 17: With a large step rearwards with the left foot, kneel down at your opponent's side and let the sword sink down very slowly until the Kissaki points at your opponent's neck. Hold the sword with the left hand and support the Mine with the right one. Stamp with the right foot on the floor while imagining stabbing towards and into the neck.

Step rearward with the left foot, kneel down and stab your opponent's neck

Turn the hip to the right while lifting the sword diagonally in front of your chest

Figure 18: Turn the right hip to the side, placing the right foot some 90° to the right. Lift the sword diagonally in front of your chest, still holding it with your left hand and supporting the back of the blade with your right hand. From there you can cut again if need should be.

Figure 19: Slide forward with your right foot while aligning the sword very slowly to your center.

Align the sword to the center

Let the sword sink down slowly for Shira Seigan

Chiburi, its style stems from Eishin Ryu

Figure 20: Let the sword sink down very slowly for Shira Seigan and control the opponent.

Figure 21: Grasp the handle with your right hand from the side and cut horizontally to your right, performing the first Chiburi. Do not move the tip away from the center line. Place the left hand on the Koiguchi.

Figure 22: Grasp the Saya at the Koiguchi and pull it in front of your lower abdomen while twisting it counterclockwise to the outside. Place the back of the blade on the scabbard near the guard, at a slanting angle.

Place the back of the blade on the Saya near the guard

Lead the tip of the blade carefully into the Koiguchi

Figure 23: Pull the sword away from the sheath quickly, until the tip falls easily into the opening of the scabbard. Let the blunt backside of the blade slide on the wood of the Saya without touching your hand. Then push the scabbard over the blade about a third of its length.

Figure 24: Finally, push the rest of the blade very slowly into the sheath while twisting it clockwise with the edge facing upwards.

Push the scabbard over the blade until about two thirds of its length are covered

25

Sit back on your left heel,
push the sword back into your belt
and secure it there

26

Stand up in a natural and relaxed
posture

Figure 25: Slide your right hand to the end of the handle and push the blade into the sheath to secure it. Bend your left knee, curl it underneath yourself and sit on top of your foot with your ankle bone sitting between the cheeks of your buttocks. Pull back your right foot and place it outwards. Bend your right knee, tuck your right foot just inside the back of your left knee and tilt your right shin outwards about 45°. This is called Tate Hiza, a posture from where you can immediately counter an attack.

Figure 26: After a short pause for concentration stand up and finish the form in a relaxed position.

15 Suemonogiri

Meaning of the form Suemonogiri: The last form described in this book is Suemonogiri. It means cutting something that is lying on a table.

You start with a step forward with the left foot, releasing the sword catch. Then you draw the sword with the second step and lift it over your head. Slide back the right foot, close your feet and lift up onto the balls of your feet. Then cut some fruit or even a grain of rice lying on a table while jumping up and coming down on both feet, performing a deep horse riding stance.

Start from a natural posture

Make a left step forward with the left foot and release the sword catch

If you are able to cut the grain of rice without scratching the table you can call yourself a true master of the sword. It is all about leverage; the jump neutralizes the momentum of the sword, so exact timing is essential – and this is the true secret or difficulty behind the technique to be mastered.

Step forward with the right foot and draw your sword

Slide back with your right foot and lift your sword for Jodan No Kamae

PERFORMING THE SUEMONOGIRI FORM

Figure 1: Stand in an upright position, feet together, the knees slightly bent. The heels touch each other and are lifted up a little from the ground. Your weight should be evenly distributed on both legs. The arms are completely relaxed hanging on the sides of the body. You should neither fix your gaze on the opponent nor look downward.

Figure 2: Make a step forward with the left foot and release the sword catch.

Figure 3: Next make a step forward with the right foot. Draw your sword and lift it over your head. At the same time pull the Saya in front of your lower abdomen.

Figure 4: After lifting the sword, grasp it with both hands. Then step back, close your feet and lift up onto the balls of your feet.

Jump down for Kibadachi and perform Shomen Uchi

Perform Chiburi, its style stems from Eishin Ryu

Figure 5: Now perform Shomen Uchi as if trying to cut up something lying on a small table in front of you. Because you should not scratch the table while cutting, it is very important to stop the blade exactly at the right point of the movement. How you can do this is described here:

Accelerate the sword only with your left hand. The right hand grasps the sword lightly, it is only used to give direction to the sword. Do not use it to stop the blade like when swinging an axe. You should stop the cut by using the momentum of the sudden lowering of your center of gravity. Therefore you must synchronize the jump down with the cut. You will probably need a lot of experience and many hours of training to perform it in the correct manner. If you stop the jump the very moment the cut is finished, the blade will stop due to the momentum. No force is needed.

Figure 6: After you have finished the cut, extend your knees and perform the first Chiburi.

Place the back of the blade on the scabbard

Push the sheath over the blade about two thirds of its length

Figure 7: The figure shows the first Noto. It is described in Chapter 4.1.1 on page 49. Place the blunt backside of the blade on the scabbard.

Figure 8: Push the scabbard over the blade until about two thirds of its length are covered.

Figure 9: Push the blade completely into the scabbard and then push both into the belt until only about two inches remain between your lower abdomen and the guard.

Resheathe the sword completely

Slide the right foot to the left and secure the sword

Figure 10: You should secure the sword by pushing it into the scabbard. At the same time slide back your right foot to the left and close your feet. The sword clips with the Habaki in the scabbard and will not fall out. First point the handle straight forward then slide your right foot back to the left.

Figure 11: To finish the form stand upright from the knees. Standing in a completely natural and relaxed posture you are ready to perform the next sword form.

Finish the form in a natural and relaxed posture

PART IV
TRANSFERRING
THE PRINCIPLES OF SWORD
COMBAT INTO AIKIDO

1 Waiting for an attack

1.1 There is no particular fighting stance

The right fighting stance with the tip of the blade facing forward

The left fighting stance with the tip of the blade facing forward

The right fighting stance with the cutting edge facing forward

The left fighting stance with the cutting edge facing forward

Neither in Aikido nor in sword fighting is there any particular fighting stance. Just as shown at the beginning of the sword techniques, Dori waits for an attack in a natural and completely relaxed posture and attitude. Only the body is turned slightly to offer the opponent as little body surface as possible for a potential attack. The sword is held losely hanging down. The arms are hanging down in a slack manner close to the body. Miyamoto Musashi called this posture the "left" and "right stance", depending on which foot is in the forward position. He considered it to be the most important stance in sword fighting.

1.2 Awase, the attack and the defense reaction are made simultaneously

Attacks with a sword are swift and very dangerous. If a defender waits until he can tell what kind of attack is about to hit him, it will be too late for him to react. In Aikido Toho Iai you do not wait for an attack. The sword form starts with a step towards the attacker. Dori's whole Ki is directed towards the attacker. In Aikido, Dori also moves at the very moment Uke moves. The attacker must not be allowed to strike a passive Dori, when it would be too late for Dori to react in an appropriate way. As soon as Uke starts his attack, Dori immediately performs Irimi and Atemi. It is not important at all for him to know what kind of attack is imminent, or if there will be an attack at all. When sword fighting in a life and death situation, there is no difference between attacking an opponent and defending oneself. When the first cut hits any of the two participants, the fight is over.

In Aikido, the simultaneity of attacking and defending, of Irimi and Atemi on sensitive parts of the body like eyes, neck, solar plexus or towards the genitals, have the effect that Uke has already lost the fight at the moment of first contact. For example: Figure 15 on page 208 shows the outer Irimi with a spearhand thrust towards the opponent's throat. This may be a reaction to Uke attacking Dori as well as an attack of Dori himself, depending on the situation. However, a distinction between the two cannot be made.

1.3 The movement for reacting to an attack is always the same

Every sword form starts the same way with a left-footed step. In Aikido, the defensive reaction also starts with Irimi and Atemi. Whether the inner or the outer

Irimi is chosen depends on the number and the position of the attackers, or the situation at the scene where the fight takes place. You will always try to slam your opponents against cars, fences, hydrants, rocks or walls – where it hurts most and will stop the attack immediately by having the potential to break limbs.

1.4 Irimi – Half a step is enough to defeat an attacker

When cutting, the blade spatially moves in one single plane. Everything lying in this plane will be struck by the blade. The defendant must not be in the zone of the blade in order to avoid being hit. Irimi brings him into a position where neither Shomen Uchi nor Kaesagiri Oroshi can strike him. For Aikido, this means that Dori can avoid straight punches or chops towards the face or upper body as well as straight kicks towards the lower body and knees, all in one single movement at once. Even attacks from the side like swings, blows with a stick and low kicks will not hit as they are in the same plane as Kaesagiri Oroshi. For the exact description of the steps for outer and inner Irimi see Chapter 2.2 on pages 26 and 28. It is extremely important to study and understand this correlation, that is to say similarity. It is the key towards a deeper understanding of Aikido. Only after Irimi and Atemi will there be any Aikido technique. They depend on factors like distance and how the attacker reacts after being hit by Dori's Atemis.

2 Fighting an opponent

2.1 The particularities of the one-edged sword

In Aikido Toho Iai forms, attacks are not blocked with the Ha. It is very sharp, but also very sensitive when it comes to chips. Cuts are being taken on the back of the blade and slid along it. Mine is very robust. In Aikido there is the expression "sword-hand" or Tegatana, which is to say that the hand and arm are moved in a manner a sword would be used. Figuratively speaking, the side of the hand the little finger is on is considered the sharp edge, whereas the side of the hand the thumb is on is meant to be the blunt back side of the sword. The inside and the outside of the lower arm are considered to be the Shinogi. Therefore, Uke's attack cannot be blocked with the side of the hand the little finger is on, pointing towards the attacker. Rather it is taken on by the upper side of the hand and deflected away from the body. This results in a decisive change in the way Dori moves. If Dori blocks an attack, he is right in front of Uke. If Dori parries the attack using the thumbside and doesn't block Uke, then, even with the first contact, he is standing in either his forward or rearward blind spot.

2.2 There are no levers in Aikido

Sword fighting means first of all quick movement, swift cuts and exact timing. Since the Katana is very sharp, no force is needed. For Aikido this denotes that there are no lever techniques at all. Levers take time and effort. If your opponent is very strong, even the best lever is useless. Moreover, with most lever techniques it is necessary to use both hands. Atemis will then no longer be feasible, and your opponent will use this opportunity for his own counterattack. When practicing in the Dojo, levers are very dangerous and are often the cause of injuries. Using swift movements in the Dojo is then almost impossible. This, however, is an indispensable precursor for practicing under realistic circumstances. Shihonage, for instance, is a good example to underline the point I wish to make. Often Dori tries to use different kinds of lever techniques in order to raise Uke's arm over his head. But Shiho Nage does not include any levers. Done properly, according to the sword form, lever techniques are not necessary at all. When practicing it slowly, the technique is completely safe and can be easily countered. The swiftness of the movement makes it dangerous. Uke often quickly reaches the limits of his capability.

2.3 Why Aikido is never wrong

Every cut with the Katana from top to the bottom is done so via the top of the head. The defender will never know whether he is going to be attacked by Shomen Uchi or by Yokomen Uchi. When not using the Katana, Shomen Uchi corresponds to a straight attack, Yokomen Uchi means an attack from the side. A straight attack might be the left straight punch of a boxer or the Maegeri of a Karateka. An attack from the side might be a kick with the heel, a Mawashi Geri or a low kick. However, Dori is neither struck by a straight attack nor by one from the side, although he has to move right into the attack without being able to know at all what kind of attack it will be.

The reason why this happens is the symmetry of Irimi. The outer Irimi, when using Shomen Uchi, will be the inner Irimi when Uke attacks with Yokomen Uchi. This is more or less an open secret and most plainly recognizable when the whole movement is performed using the sword. The sequence of footsteps and the movement of the hands have to correspond with each other, no matter whether the movement is done with or without the sword. It is important to know that the stab with the sword towards the throat is done with the blade in an upward position that will turn into a cut if the aim has been missed. That is why the first Irimi is always accompanied by two Atemis.

3 Symmetry in Aikido

The outer Irimi when being attacked with Shomen Uchi is turned into an inner Irimi when being attacked with Yokomen Uchi:
The outer Irimi is shown in the left column (Figures 5,7,9), the inner Irimi in the right column (Figures 6, 8, 10).

The outer Irimi when being attacked from the front equals the inner Irimi when being attacked from the side:
The outer Irimi is shown in the left column (Figures 11, 13, 15 & 17), the inner Irimi in the right column (Figures 12, 14, 16 & 18).

Shomen Uchi, Ai Hanmi, left foot in front as starting position

Yokomen Uchi, Ai Hanmi, left foot in front as starting position

Shomen Uchi, step to the right with a stab towards the throat

Yokomen Uchi, step to the right with a stab towards the throat

Shomen Uchi, the left foot is drawn back to the right foot, at the same time cut to the throat

Yokomen Uchi, the left foot is drawn back to the right foot, at the same time cut to the throat

Jodan No Tsuki, expecting an attack from Ai Hanmi stance with the left foot in front

Mawashi Uchi, expecting an attack from Ai Hanmi stance with the left foot in front

Jodan No Tsuki, half step to the right with a left hand Atemi to the armpit

Mawashi Uchi, half step to the right with a left hand Atemi to the face

Jodan No Tsuki, without changing stance, followed by a right-handed chop to the throat

Mawashi Uchi, without changing stance, followed by a right-handed chop to the throat

Jodan No Tsuki, left foot is drawn to the right foot, at the same time right knife-hand strike to the neck

Mawashi Uchi, left foot drawn to the right foot, at the same time Uraken Uchi (strike with the back of the fist) to Uke's face

The inner Irimi when being attacked with Shomen Uchi turns into outer Irimi when being attacked with Yokomen Uchi:
The inner Irimi is shown in the left column (Figures 19, 21, 23), the outer Irimi is shown in the right column (Figures 20, 22, 24).

Shomen Uchi, Gyaku Hanmi stance with left foot in front as a starting position

Yokomen Uchi, Gyaku Hanmi stance with left foot in front as a starting position

Shomen Uchi, side-step to the right and back with a stab to the throat

Yokomen Uchi, side-step to the right and back with a stab to the throat

Shomen Uchi, left foot is drawn to the right foot, at the same time cut to the throat

Yokomen Uchi, left foot is drawn to the right foot, at the same time cut to the throat

The inner Irimi when being attacked from the front equals the outer Irimi when being attacked from the side:
The inner Irimi is shown in the left column (Figures 25, 27, 29 & 31), the outer Irimi is shown in the right column (Figures 26, 28, 30 & 32).

Jodan No Tsuki, expecting an attack in a right-footed forward stance

Mawashi Uchi, expecting an attack with Mawashi Uchi in right-footed forward stance

Jodan No Tsuki, half step back with right foot and right-handed chop to the throat

Mawashi Uchi, half step back with right foot and right-handed chop to the throat

Jodan No Tsuki, without changing stance, followed by a second Atemi with the left hand to the chin

Mawashi Uchi, without changing stance, followed by a left-handed knuckle punch to the ribs

Jodan No Tsuki, left foot is drawn to the right foot, at the same time right-handed Uraken Uchi to the face

Mawashi Uchi, left foot is drawn to the right, at the same time right knife-hand strike to the neck.

There are more symmetrical movements contained in the individual steps of combinations of the four starting positions in sword fighting. These are not, however, covered here in this book.

PART V
THE AIKIDO
TECHNIQUES

Figure 1: Both partners stand opposite each other with both leading with the right foot. The position is completely natural with relaxed arms and shoulders. There is no specific posture of the arms like in some other martial arts. The knees are slightly bent. The heel of the back foot is lifted up a little from the ground. In this way, the weight of the body is shifted forward. This is the same stance as is used in sword combat. The attacker cannot deduce the type of defense that will be used.

Figure 2: Uke makes a sliding step forward and grasps Dori's wrist. This is a very dangerous attack because the forearm is blocked and Dori can get hit by a left cross. Dori makes a half step to the right out of the line of attack with a small turn to the left called Irimi. Only because of this, Uke cannot use his rearward hand to strike.

Figure 3: Dori completes his turn to the left with Tenkan Ashi and leads Uke into his original direction. In this position he can hit Uke in the face with his right hand, pushing towards him, if Uke lets go of the hand.

Figure 4: Dori makes a large step to the right into Kibadachi still facing Uke. He swings his right arm in a circular motion up to the right. Due to this Uke will be pulled strongly and turned to his left. At the same time Dori can hit Uke's liver with Atemi.

Figure 5: The pull on the arm, in combination with a large step to the left in the direction of the Uke's left heel, throws him forward and off balance.

Figure 6: After losing his balance, the attacker will be thrown to the ground with a large right step. When training, just pull the arm in order not to injure your partner. In a real fight you would thrust the shoulder on the ground and break it. This is very dangerous.

Figure 7: On the mat you can pin down your partner's elbow with the weight of your body. On the street you can deliver a knife-hand strike to the neck or break the elbow.

Put your left foot next the right one and push with your right hand towards your opponent's face

Step to the right into Kibadachi for Kuzushi and deliver a left Atemi to the attacker's liver

Make a large step about 45° to your left while pulling Uke's arm

Make a second large step to the right and throw Uke onto the ground

Uke is pinned down on the ground by pressure on his elbow

2 Shomen Uchi Ikkyo

Normally Dori blocks the strike with the outside of his forearm and pushes Uke's arm with both hands forward and up. This movement is wrong and very dangerous for Dori, because he uses both hands while Uke's rearward hand is free to deliver a punch. To do so Uke has only got to relax his forearm and turn his hip to the right.

If you study the sword form, you can clearly see that the blade of the opponent is not blocked but slightly deflected to the side, using the Mine, while Dori turns his body to the left. There is no breaking power and no pushing against the attacker. In Aikido the movement is exactly the same as in sword combat. Without blocking, Dori brings the partner into the original direction to his side and hits him in the face with his other hand at the moment of contact. After that Uke is pulled forward and thrown off balance. Then he is forced on to the ground where he is pinned down by the weight of Dori's body.

Figure 1: Both partners face each other, leading with their right foot. The position is completely natural with relaxed arms and shoulders. There is no specific posture of the arms like in some other martial arts. The knees are slightly bent. The heel of the back foot is a lifted up a little. In this way, the weight of the body is shifted forward. This is the same stance as used in sword combat. The attacker cannot deduce the type of defense that will be used.

Right-footed fighting position Ai Hanmi

Half step to the right with Irimi, right Atemi to the face

Without moving your feet, deliver a second Atemi to your opponent's face

Follow with a third Atemi to his face while pulling the left foot to the right

Step to the right, deliver a left Atemi to his liver and break Uke's balance

Make a large step towards Uke's left heel while pulling his right arm

Make a large step to the right and bring Uke down onto the ground

Uke is pinned down by the weight of Dor's body on his elbow. An Atemi to the neck is possible

Figure 2: When training usually Uke attacks with Shomen Uchi. This would not happen in a real fight but it is safer for the partner while practicing. With more experience you should use Jodan Tsuki, because it is much more realistic in terms of the street fight. Dori makes a half step to the right and turns his body a little to the left. This is called Irimi. Now he is completely out of the line of attack but can reach Uke's face with a right-handed punch.

Figure 3: Without changing the position Dori delivers a second Atemi with his left hand into Uke's face.

Figure 4: While pulling the left foot to the right Dori pushes down Uke's right arm. Simultaneously he launches a third Atemi to his face. Therefore the attacker has no chance to get the initiative back in order to continue his attack.

Figure 5: Both hands cut to the middle of Uke's belly. The right hand strikes to the groin and swings under Uke's arm. The palm of the hand is facing upwards and with a step to the right the forearm pushes Uke's arm up and to the right. At the same time the left hand launches an Atemi at Uke's lower ribs. Both the push with the right arm and the strike to the ribs will easily and readily turn Uke to the left .

Figure 6: Dori grasps Uke's right arm by the elbow and the wrist and makes a large step towards Uke's left heel. He swings both hands up and down and simultaneously pushes with his left hand and pulls with his right one. This movement throws Uke forward and off balance.

Figure 7: After breaking his balance Uke is thrown to the right with a large step. While training you should pull Uke. On the street you should push the shoulder of Uke onto the ground in order to break it.

Figure 8: On the mat Uke is pinned down by his elbow with Dori using the weight of his body. In a street fight you can deliver a knife-hand strike to the neck or break the limb.

3   Gyaku Hanmi Katate Dori No Kaiten Nage

Kaiten Nage means to throw the opponent by using a turning action. This is a very dangerous technique when performed in a normal urban environment because there are many obstacles around which can cause serious injury when Uke is hurled against them. In the Dojo it is safe to train and is therefore often taught to beginners. The basis of the technique is the sword form Ushirogiri.

Figure 1: You should face your partner in a relaxed stance with slightly bent knees. The toes are pointing towards Uke while the heel of the rear foot is lifted up a little. This brings the weight of your body towards him. There is no special position for the hands like in the other martial arts. The stance is exactly the same as is used in sword combat. The attacker has no idea what kind of defence he is facing.

Figure 2: Uke attacks with Gyaku Hanmi Katate Dori. This is a very dangerous threat because in a real fight the aggressor can kick at the knee, and there is no way to avoid it by stepping back. Therefore Dori makes a half step called Irimi to his right side and simultaneously launches a right-handed punch to the face.

Fighting stance Ai Hanmi – right leg leading

Half step back to the right with Atemi to the face

Turn with a Tenkan Ashi by the left foot, and use an Atemi again at the face

While turning Uke about 180° Dori steps to his side with both feet and delivers an Uraken Uchi into Uke's face

Dori steps under Uke's armpit while delivering an Atemi to the ribs and to the groin and turns his body about 180° to the right

Dori makes a step back behind Uke, breaks his balance and launches a strike with the palm of his hand at his face

Dori puts pressure on the neck while lifting Uke's arm up

Because of the threat of a knee strike, Uke has to escape with a forward roll

Figure 3: Dori makes a turn to his left and brings Uke into his original direction while delivering an Atemi at his face.

Figure 4: Dori pulls his right foot back to his left foot and then to the right into a deep Kibadachi. Without pausing he places his left foot to the right so that he is then standing on Uke's left side with both feet together. Uke turns about 180° to his left and is hit by an Atemi into his face with the backhand of the fist.

Figure 5: Dori launches a left elbow strike to Uke's ribs, lifts his right arm over his head and makes a large step under Uke's armpit. To avoid any possible attacks to his back, he hits the groin of Uke with a backhand strike while stepping through.

Figure 6: In order to throw Uke off balance, Dori turns his body about 180° to his right and launches a double knife-hand strike to the belly and to the throat of Uke. Uke has to avoid the devastating blow by pushing back the striking hand. Dori uses the impetus of the push to bring Uke downwards and makes a large left step back. Uke loses his balance and falls forward where he is hit by a strike with the palm of the hand coming up at the face.

Figure 7: Without stopping the movement, Dori delivers a knife-hand strike to Uke's neck. Because Uke cannot protect his neck, he has to duck deep. There he is held by a grip on his neck while his left arm is lifted up. This is a very uncomfortable position where he is open to a devastating knee strike to the side of his head or body.

Figure 8: The only possibility to escape this awkward and dangerous situation is to roll forward. In a real fight Dori pushes Uke with full force in any direction against a wall, a car or some other obstacle in the urban environment.

4 Ai Hanmi Katate Dori Shiho Nage

Shiho Nage literally means a throw in four directions, but it is also known as throwing when using a sword. The first important thing is that you can throw your opponent wherever you want, and this is essential in a life or death combat situation. You can throw him against other attackers or different obstacles. The second thing to keep in mind is that you have to move like in sword combat. There you cut a Kiriage, turn round about 180° and, without pausing, you cut Kaesagiri Oroshi. If it is done in this manner, the technique will work. Therefore it is important to practice the technique with a sword or a Bokken first and with your partner later on.

There are two points to remember. The first point is the step to the side, not forward. And you cut twice diagonally, not straight. These two points are very important to keep in mind when you start practicing with a partner for the first time. If it is done in an incorrect manner, Shiho Nage will not work in a real street fight. On the contrary, it will lead you into a very bad situation.

Figure 1: Both partners stand opposite each other with both leading with the right foot.

Fighting stance Ai Hanmi – right leg leading

Uke grasps Dori's right wrist, and delivers a powerful cross. Perform Irimi to the right with a left-handed Atemi to the face

Pulling his left foot behind his right, Dori pushes towards Uke's face

Uke is thrown off balance by continuing the impetus of the force to the right

Stepping to the side while pulling the arm diagonally in front of the forehead

Throwing Uke by cutting down diagonally to the left after a 180° turn to the right

Control Uke by putting pressure on his wrist

Figure 2: Uke grasps Dori's right wrist, and delivers a powerful cross. Dori makes a half step back to the right, just like the Irimi in the sword form. He turns his palm upward and pulls his arm back. Therefore Uke cannot use his rear hand, but he can be hit by a left Atemi. Note that, despite stepping back, Dori has turned his body towards his partner.

Figure 3: Dori places his left foot behind his right one. Leaning forward and using the weight of his body he pushes his right hand towards Uke's face. To avoid the Atemi, Uke has to press it back.

Figure 4: Dori uses the force of the push carried out by Uke and deflects it to the right, while stepping to the same side himself. This movement is the key to the technique. Uke has the feeling of falling into a big hole. Pulling on his arm is completely wrong.

Figure 5: Dori makes a step to the side, not forward, by crossing his left foot in front of his right one, and pulls Uke's arm in the same direction in front of his forehead. Without pausing Dori turns his body about 180°, always keeping the hand in front of his forehead.

Figure 6: After turning, Dori makes a large step forward with his right foot, and just like the cut in the sword form, he pulls Uke's arm diagonally to his left. This kind of throw is very dangerous to the shoulder, especially if your partner is inexperienced. Try to practice Shiho Nage in the correct manner, even if you have to perform it very slowly.

Figure 7: You are free to throw Uke wherever you want to or bring him down to control him by putting pressure on his wrist. Note that you have to line up alongside your partner in order to avoid being kicked on your head.

5 Gyaku Hanmi Katate Dori No Shiho Nage

The difference between this Gyaku Hanmi technique and Ai Hanmi Shiho Nage is only the kind of attack. The rest of the technique is the same. But the difference between the performance described here and the way it is normally practiced is very substantial.

Figure 1: Both partners face each other, leading with the right foot. The position is completely natural with relaxed arms and shoulders. There is no specific posture of the arms like in some other martial arts. The knees are slightly bent. The heel of the back foot is lifted up a little. In this way, the weight of the body is shifted forward. This is the same stance as used in sword combat. The attacker cannot deduce the type of defense that will be used, since the posture of the latter does not give any clues.

Figure 2: Uke makes a step forward with the left foot and grasps Dori's right hand in order to deliver a kick or a punch. Dori steps to the left side and turns his body a little to the right. This movement is called Irimi. He moves both hands in a circular manner in front of his body. The right one protects his face against a punch, the left one protects his lower body against a kick.

Ai Hanmi, the fighting stance with right foot leading

Make a half step to the right with Irimi. The left hand protects you from a kick

While controlling Uke's arm, Dori places his right foot behind his left and delivers a left Atemi to Uke's face

With a large step to the left Dori draws Uke off balance and delivers a right Atemi to his kidney

Stepping to the side while turning about 180° to his left, Dori pulls Uke's arm over his head

Uke is forced to arch his back and is thrown hard onto the ground

Uke is controlled by the weight of Dori's body on his wrist

The figure shows the method of holding the hand while executing the Shiho Nage throw

Figure 3: Dori puts his right foot behind his left one and delivers a left Atemi to Uke's face while controlling Uke's left arm. Therefore he cannot use his rear hand for a counter strike.

Figure 4: Without pausing Dori makes a large step to the left into Kibadachi and pulls Uke's arm in front of his center. Uke is turned to his right and is unable to regain his balance.

Figure 5: The very moment Uke finishes his turning motion, but has not yet regained his balance, Dori makes a crossover step to his left while pulling Uke's forearm to his forehead. Immediately he turns his body about 180° to his left still holding both hands on his forehead. This movement forces Uke to arch his back and brings him completely off balance, so that he is thrown very hard onto the ground.

Figure 6: The figure shows the very uncomfortable position Uke is in just before the throw. Note that Uke is not thrown by force of the hand but by a large step towards his right heel. It is very important to hold both hands in front of your brow while turning, otherwise you can step into a vacuum, giving your opponent the chance to pull you back.

Figure 7: You are free to throw your opponent in any direction you want, maybe against some other opponents, against different obstacles or into a free space for a safe forward roll in the Dojo. You can also take him down and control him by putting all the weight of your body on his wrist.

Figure 8: The picture depicts the method of holding Uke's hand while throwing him. The grip is the same as when holding a sword. Note the open index finger with which pressure is applied to a vital pressure point called Neiguan on the inside of the forearm.

6 Gyaku Hanmi Nikyo

When watching the technique, people usually think that Nikyo works by applying a leverage on the wrist. But in a real fight it is not possible to catch the fist of an aggressor in order to perform the technique properly. Because leverage takes time to work, there is always the risk of a counter strike. And if the enemy is very strong, leverage may be not enough to subdue him.

Looking at the sword form, you can see that in reality there is actually no leverage applied on the wrist. The opponent cannot draw the sword and has to let go of the Tsuka because of the pressure on his wrist. After that he is controlled by the blade. In Aikido the blade is replaced by the Atemi. In this case the Atemi is a kick to the side of the knee (Yoko Geri). The opponent has to pull his leg back and therefore he loses his balance. This is the reason way he can be brought effortlessly to the ground.

Figure 1: You should face your partner in a relaxed stance with knees slightly bent. The toes are pointing toward him while the heel of the rear foot is lifted up a little. This brings the weight of your body towards him.

There is no special position for the hands like in some other martial arts. The stance is completely the same as is used in sword combat. The attacker has no idea what kind of defence he is facing.

Figure 2: Uke grasps Dori's hand after stepping forward. Dori performs Irimi by stepping back to the right. Simultaneously he turns his palm upwards and draws his forearm in front of his belly. Due to this movement, Uke is brought into his original direction and cannot use his rear hand for a counter while at the same time being open for an Atemi to his face himself.

Figure 3: Dori makes a large turn to his left, stepping back with his left leg, and continues pulling his forearm towards his belly. This is an excellent technique to free the hand, but it is impossible for Uke to let it go, because Dori's fist is so close to his face. Therefore Uke has to follow Dori's movement.

Fighting stance Ai Hanmi - right leg leading

Half step back to the right while leading Uke forward

Turning to his left with Tenkan Ashi, Dori delivers an Atemi to Uke's face

Still leading Uke forward, Dori steps to his side and launches a second Atemi

Dori puts his left foot behind the right one and puts all his weight onto Uke's elbow. A jab with the fingers to the eyes is possible at any time

Feigning a right-footed kick sideways to the knee, Dori forces Uke down

Dori grasps the elbow from below and can launch a straight kick

Like Ikkyo Ura, Dori turns his body with Tai Sabaki and forces Uke onto the ground

A powerful technique to immobilize Uke with arms crossed

The method of holding the wrist shown in Figure

Figure 4: Dori pulls his right foot back to his left foot and then goes into a deep Kibadachi to the right, Dori keeps his hands in front of his navel to prevent Uke from turning towards him. It is important for Dori to be alongside Uke, not in front of him. In this position, Dori delivers an Atemi to Uke's face and then blocks the elbow with his left hand, forcing Uke to remain in this position.

Figure 5: Dori turns to the left sharply, stepping with his left foot behind the right one, stretching his body up and pulling Uke's hand to his right shoulder, thumb pointing towards his chest. With his right hand, Dori delivers an Atemi to the eye, and with the same movement he grasps the wrist, putting his forearm over Uke's.

Figure 6: Feigning a right-footed kick sideways to the knee, Dori steps to the right into a deep Kibadachi. Losing his balance because he has to protect his leg, Uke is brought to the ground without the need for any force on his wrist.

Figure 7: Dori launches a straight kick with his left leg and grasps the elbow from below in the same manner as Ikkyo.

Figure 8: With Tai Sabaki, turning the body with one step forward and a second one back, Dori brings his partner to the ground.

Figure 9: Dori falls down onto his knees at the side of Uke, sitting on his own toes. With a straight back Dori catches Uke's arm between his forearms, which he holds in a crossed manner in front of his chest. While lifting the shoulder about two inches above the ground, in order to prevent Uke escaping by simply rolling forward, Dori pushes the straight arm towards Uke's neck. This immobilizes the partner without causing any pain. It is just the weight that keeps him down.

7 Ai Hanmi Nikyo

As described in the previous chapter, Nikyo is not a technique that inflicts pain by applying leverage to the wrist, because again the sword form shows that the opponent is able to loosen his grip. The control by the blade is replaced by yet another kick to the side of the knee, forcing Uke to protect it. If he does so, which is strongly recommended, he is thrown off balance and is brought to the ground without the need for any force.

Figure 1: Both partners face each other, leading with the right leg forward. Your posture is completely relaxed. The knees are slightly bent. The weight of the body is shifted a little forward by lifting up the heel of the right foot. There is no special position for the arms as is in some other martial arts. The position is exactly the same as is normally used in sword combat.

Figure 2: Uke grasps Dori's wrist with the intention of attacking with a straight punch to the face or a straight kick. To avoid this, Dori makes a half step back to his right, simultaneously pulling his arm back to his belly, palm facing upwards.

Figure 3: After that, Dori turns to his left, stepping with his left foot behind his right one and uses the impetus of his hip to push towards Uke's face with his right hand.

Fighting stance Ai Hanmi – right leg leading

The partner attacks grasping Dori's wrist intending to launch a punch to the face

3

After stepping back to the right, Dori puts his left foot behind the right one and thrusts to Uke's face with his right hand

4

Without pausing, Dori makes a second Tenkan Ashi in order to neutralize the pressure applied by Uke

5

Feigning a sideways kick, Dori pivots with his hips to the left and applies Nikyo

6

After a straight kick with the left foot, Dori grasps the elbow as if performing Ikkyo

7

Pulling the arm while pushing down on the elbow, Dori brings Uke down

8

A powerful technique to immobilize Uke with crossed arms

Figure 4: Uke has to push back to avoid getting hit. Dori uses this impetus to draw Uke off balance. To do so, he turns his right hand counterclockwise under Uke's forearm and then in front of his brow, holding the elbow deep and the palm towards his head. Simultaneously, he puts his left hand on the fingers of Uke's right hand and grabs them. At the same time, Dori makes a Tenkan Ashi with his right foot behind his left one.

Figure 5: Feigning a sideways kick, Dori steps to his left into a deep Kibadachi. Without pausing he turns his hips to the left while cutting diagonally to Uke's neck with his right hand. Without using leverage, Uke is pushed back, he loses his balance and falls on his knees.

Figure 6: To maintain control Dori delivers a straight kick (Maegeri) and steps forward while grasping the elbow from below in the same manner as used when performing Ikkyo.

Figure 7: With Tai Sabaki, turning the body with one step forward and a second back, Dori brings his partner to the ground.

Figure 8: Dori falls down onto his knees at the side of Uke, sitting on his own toes. With a straight back he catches Uke's arm between his own forearms, which he holds crossed in front of his chest. While lifting the shoulder about two inches above the ground, in order to prevent Uke escaping by simply rolling forward, Dori pushes the straight arm towards Uke's neck. This immobilizes the partner without causing any pain. It is just the weight that keeps him down.

8 Jodan Tsuki No Sankyo

When seeing Sankyo for the first time, people often believe that the technique works with leverage. But there is no way to catch the fist of a skilled striker and apply a twisting lock on the wrist.

Again, in the sword form there is no sign of leverage being applied. All you can see is the movement of the body, a thrust to the heart and a cut to the neck of the aggressor. In Aikido, the thrust with the sword equates to a punch to the Adam's apple, and the cut equates to a devastating knife-hand strike to the neck of the opponent. To avoid these strikes the aggressor has to protect himself and therefore he loses his balance and it is easy to bring Uke down without the use of any force.

Figure 1: Both partners face each other, leading with the right foot. The position is completely natural with relaxed arms and shoulders. There is no specific position for the arms as is in some other martial arts. Your knees are slightly bent. The heel of the back foot is lifted up a little. This shifts the weight of the body forward. This is the same stance as is used in sword combat. The attacker has no idea what kind of defense he is facing by looking at the posture.

Figure 2: The opponent attacks the defender's face with a straight punch. Because this is very dangerous, you should use the open hand while training with your partner in order to avoid injury. Dori leaves the line of attack with a half step to the left while turning his body a little to his right. It is important that your toes point towards Uke. The punch should not be blocked, but deflected to the side with the outside of the forearm. Simultaneously Dori launches a knife-hand strike at Uke's neck. The force of the strike is tremendous, because Uke is still pushing forward.

Figure 3: While pulling his right foot to the left and turning to the right, Dori grasps Uke's forearm with both hands. He lowers his body and shifts his weight to the right into a deep Kibadachi. Therefore, Uke is thrown off balance and cannot counter with his rear hand.

Figure 4: Uke has to follow the movement and turn his thumb downwards towards the ground, otherwise his elbow would be broken. Dori increases the pressure and presses the edge of his right hand against the little finger side of the arm. The left hand grasps the side of Uke's hand from the inside.

Fighting position Ai Hanmi – leading with the right foot

Half step to the left with Irimi and Atemi to the neck

Turn to the right while attacking the elbow

In order to avoid a broken elbow Uke is forced to make a large step forward and loses his balance

Dori steps in front of Uke and delivers an Atemi to the neck

Kibadachi to the left with a strike with the palm of the hand to the chin

A knife-handed strike causes Uke to duck and lose his balance

Uke is thrown down by pulling and pushing on his elbow

Holding the little finger is the key to controlling even the strongest opponent

Figure 5: Dori steps back to the center line with both feet while turning his body to the left. He pulls the right arm of Uke down to his left side and delivers a devastating punch to his Adam's apple. To avoid the punch Uke has to arch his body back.

Figure 6: Using the backward movement of Uke, Dori makes a large step to the left behind Uke into a deep Kibadachi. Simultaneously, he pulls Uke's right arm down. Surprised by this Uke loses his balance and falls forward. Here he will be hit on his chin by a powerful strike with the palm of the hand.

Figure 7: Uke has to protect his face to avoid a knock out. After that he is forced to duck down deep caused by receiving a tremendous knife-hand strike to his neck, and loses his balance again.

Figure 8: With his right hand Dori pushes Uke's elbow down while pulling the latter's wrist with his own left hand. In combination with a large turn of the body to the right called Tenkan Ashi, Dori forces Uke down to the ground. Not the pushing but the pulling is the reason why Uke cannot counter the technique.

Figure 9: In order to immobilize Uke, Dori kneels down on Uke's right and lays Uke's arm over his left thigh. His right hand slides from the elbow down to Uke's little finger and grasps it. Then he uses his left elbow as a hook to support the pressing motion. Dori lifts Uke's shoulder a little off the ground, thus preventing Uke from escaping by simply doing a forward roll.

9 Jodan Tsuki No Kote Kaeshi

Kote Kaeshi means to bend or twist the Kote back. The Kote is the Samurai's protection of the upper forearm, made from metal. Most people believe that Kote Kaeshi is a kind of wrist lock. But in a real fight it is not possible to catch the opponent's wrist and force him down by applying a wrist lock. The most important thing is not the technique per se but the footwork and the body movement. As described earlier in the sword form you cross the center line several times. These steps and the twisting back of the forearm force the enemy down very effectively.

Figure 1: You should face your partner in a relaxed stance with slightly bent knees. The toes are directed towards him while the heel is lifted up slightly. This brings the weight of your body towards him. There is no special position for the hands as is in some other martial arts. The stance is completely the same as is used in sword combat. The attacker has no idea what kind of defence he is facing.

Figure 2: Uke attacks with a straight punch to the face. Dori leaves the center line with a half step back to the right. He turns his body about 45° towards the attacker and delivers a punch to the face with his right hand.

Figure 3: Without moving the feet, Dori delivers a second punch to Uke's face. Simultaneously, he raises his right hand over his head.

Figure 4: Dori pulls his left foot to the right and turns his body sharply to the left, using the impetus of the turning movement to deliver a hard punch using the back hand to the face. Uke has to protect himself from being struck in the face. Therefore, Dori brings his right hand to the right upper arm and pushes it to his right side.

Figure 5: Dori makes a large step left behind Uke and launches a strike with his left knuckle to his right eye. Simultaneously he leads Uke's right arm forward and up.

Figure 6: Dori turns completely to the right and pushes Uke's right arm forward without pulling it to the right. Uke has to escape with a step and a turn to the right, otherwise he will be hit by a devastating strike to the kidney with his right elbow. Note that Uke has to move to avoid this strike. He is not pulled to the right.

Fighting stance Ai Hanmi - right foot leading

Half step back to the right while delivering a punch with the right hand

Second Atemi with the left hand without moving the feet

Third Atemi with a punch by the back of the hand to the aggressor's face while pulling the left foot to the right

Step to the left with a strike to the right eye

Turn the body to the right while grasping the forearm

Step left to the rear with a turn to the left while twisting the forearm outwards

Uke will be turned on his belly with a large step towards the head

Uke is controlled by applying pressure on his elbow and shoulder

Figure 7: While Uke is about to attack again, Dori makes a step to the left rear and turns to his left while twisting Uke's forearm outward with both hands.

Figure 8: Uke loses his balance and falls down onto his back. Note that a forward fall by Uke is only for show. In reality Uke has many possibilities to counter with a throw or a strike when he is able to fall forward. In a real fight you should twist the forearm hard to the outside using your right elbow for a brutal strike to the face. After that you have to roll Uke on his belly with a large step with the right leg towards his head.

Figure 9: Dori kneels down on both knees at Uke's side and grasps the wrist with his right hand. Dori's left elbow supports his right hand and pushes the arm to Uke's neck using the weight of his body. Dori lifts Uke's shoulder a little off the ground, thus preventing Uke from escaping by simply doing a forward roll.

10 Shomen Uchi No Irimi Nage

One of the most interesting techniques in Aikido is Irimi Nage. There are different methods of performing Irimi Nage in the existing Aikido schools. The key to understanding the technique is to know that all of them are correct. There are many ways of performing Irimi Nage, but there is only one principle, and this is shown in the sword form Tsume.

Figure 1: Both partners face each other, both leading with the right foot.

Figure 2: Uke makes a right-footed sliding step forward and attacks with a Shomen Uchi or a straight punch to the face. Dori leaves the line of attack with a half step to the right, turning a little to the left, and delivers two Atemi from below to Uke's face. The first one with the right hand and the second one with the left.

Figure 3: With a sharp turn of the hip to the left Dori puts his left foot behind his right one and uses this momentum to deliver a third punch with the back of the hand to Uke's face. Simultaneously, he pushes Uke's right arm down and puts his own right hand on Uke's upper arm. He makes a large left step behind Uke while leading his right arm to the right side of his body.

Fighting stance Ai Hanmi – right foot leading

Half step to the right and deliver two Atemi into Uke's face

While pulling the left foot to the right deliver a third Atemi with a backfist strike

Dori steps behind Uke and grasps his neck with his left hand and the elbow with his right one

While turning sharply to his right, Dori leads Uke's head to his right shoulder

Dori uses his right arm pushing back Uke's head with the thumb facing downwards

Using both arms like a scissor, Dori slams Uke very hard onto the ground

Close your fingers and choke him if necessary

Figure 4: After stepping behind Uke, Dori grasps him at the rear of his neck with the left hand and, in order to avoid an elbow strike, he pushes the right elbow towards his face. Uke has to push his elbow down to avoid being thrown backwards.

Figure 5: Dori uses this momentum and turns sharply to his right, leading Uke's head to his right shoulder. Note that it is important to control Uke's neck with the thumb to avoid a head butt and to move behind him for proper control.

Figure 6: As a result of the spinning movement Uke loses his balance completely. At this point Dori makes a large right step in the direction of Uke's left heel, using his right arm, thumb down, to push Uke's head back. Simultaneously he pushes forward with his left hand. This movement creates a strong twisting pressure on Uke's neck. Therefore you have to be extremely careful with your partner while practicing.

Figure 7: Uke, having been pushed back, loses his balance and falls onto the mat.

Figure 8: In a life or death situation, i.e. when being attacked with a knife, it is possible to close your fingers and choke the aggressor or even break the neck.

11 Shomen Uchi Uchi Kaiten Sankyo

In this chapter Uchi Kaiten Sankyo is described when Uke attacks with Ai Hanmi Shomen Uchi. The basis of the technique is the sword form Sanpo.

Figure 1: Both partners face each other, both leading with the right foot. The position is completely natural with arms and shoulders relaxed. There is no specific position for the arms as is in some other martial arts. The knees are slightly bent. The heel of the back foot lifted up a little. This shifts the weight of the body forward. This is the same stance as is used in sword combat. The attacker has no idea what kind of attack he is facing by looking at the posture.

Figure 2: Uke makes a sliding step and grasps Dori's wrist with his right hand. Dori leaves the line of attack with a half step to the left, grasps Uke's elbow and twists the forearm to the outside while turning to the right. If Uke does not follow, his elbow will be broken.

Figure 3: Dori continues turning to the right and pulls Uke's arm to the outside. Uke must follow the movement to avoid breaking his limb and is therefore pushed forward in his original direction.

Figure 4: Uke is turned 180° while Dori steps to his side with both feet. Dori pulls the arm of Uke towards himself and over his head. Because of this, Uke is unable to counter.

Figure 5: Now Dori makes a large step under Uke's arm and turns his body about 180° to the right. To do so Dori loosens the grip on Uke's wrist a little in order to let it rotate freely.

Figure 6: Dori puts pressure on the little finger of Uke's right hand with his palm while stepping to his left side, behind Uke, into a deep Kibadachi.

Figure 7: After that Dori pulls his right foot to the left, pushing up with his legs, back straight and forces Uke to stand on his toes by pushing his elbow into the sky. In this position Uke is unable to counter with a kick or a strike.

Fighting stance Ai Hanmi – leading with the right foot

Make a half step to the left with Irimi and try to break your opponent's elbow

Turn your body to the right with Tenkan Ashi while pulling Uke forward

Turn Uke 180° and lift the arm over your head

Make a big step under the arm of Uke and turn 180°

Apply Sankyo by twisting the wrist of Uke towards his face

7 Throw Uke off balance by pushing his arm straight up

8 Pull the arm down and deliver a strike with the palm of the hand at Uke's chin

9 Deliver a knife-hand strike to the neck

10 Pull the arm while putting pressure on the elbow to bring Uke down

11 Pin Uke on the ground by holding his little finger

Figure 8: Pulling the arm of Uke down, Dori makes another large step to his left into a deep Kibadachi. Simultaneously, he delivers a strike with the palm of his hand at Uke's face. Uke has to protect his face and is therefore unable to follow the movement. Without pausing Dori delivers a hard knife-hand strike to the unprotected neck. Therefore Uke has to duck in order to avoid a knock-out and loses his balance.

Figure 9: With his right hand Dori pushes Uke's elbow down while pulling the wrist with his left hand. In combination with a large turn of the body to the right, called Tenkan Ashi, Dori forces Uke down to the ground. Not the pushing but the pulling is the reason why Uke cannot counter the technique.

Figure 10: In order to immobilize Uke, Dori kneels down on Uke's right knee and lays Uke's arm over his own left thigh. He slides with his right hand from the elbow down to the little finger and grasps it. Then he uses his left elbow as a hook to support the pressing motion. To prevent Uke from escaping by simply rolling forward, Dori lifts Uke's shoulder a little.

12 Yokomen Uchi No Shiho Nage

In this chapter Shiho Nage is described when the opponent attacks with Yokomen Uchi. In a real fight this kind of attack is a big problem, because it can be delivered from different angles. Studying the form Shiho is the key to understanding the way of finding a method to defend against this threat.

Figure 1: Both partners face each other, both leading with the left foot. The position is completely relaxed. The knees are slightly bent. The body weight is shifted a little forward by lifting up the heel of the right foot. There is no special position for the arms as is in some other martial arts. The position is exactly the same as is normally used in sword combat.

Figure 2: Uke makes a large step forward with the right foot and delivers a punch to Dori's left temple. Dori moves to the right with a half step. Simultaneously, he turns to his left and delivers an Atemi from below to the chin of the opponent with his left hand and a strike to the groin with his right hand.

Fighting stance Ai Hanmi – left leg leading

Half step forward to the right, Atemi with the left hand to Uke's face

While stepping with his left foot behind the right one, Dori delivers a strike to Uke's face with the back of the hand

Dori is thrown off balance by pulling to the right

With a crossover step to the right Dori turns about 180° to the right

Uke is thrown on his back

Uke is controlled by the weight of Dori's body on his wrist

Figure 3: Dori pulls his left hand back to protect his face, puts his left foot behind his right one and strikes with the back of the hand to Uke's face. The power of the strike comes by moving the hip.

Figure 4: Without pausing Dori grasps Uke's arm with both hands and pulls him to the right. Using the weight of his own body he makes a large step to the right into a deep Kibadachi. At the same time he delivers a devasting Atemi to Uke's right kidney.

Figure 5: Uke is turned to the left and loses his balance completely. Just before he regains it, Dori makes a step to the right and pulls Uke's arm in front of his forehead. It is very important to pull the arm to the outside.

Figure 6: After the step, Dori turns about 180° to his right. Still holding Uke's arm in front of his brow, he forces Uke to arch his back.

Figure 7: You are free to throw your opponent in any direction you want, maybe against some other opponents, different obstacles or into a free space for a safe forward roll in the Dojo. You can also take him down and control him by the weight of your body on his wrist.

AIKIDO – **TOHO IAI**

13 Yokomen Uchi Gokyo

In this chapter Gokyo from Gyaku Hanmi Yokomen Uchi will be described. The basis of the technique is the sword form Nukiawase.

It is worth practicing this technique often in training because it is decisive when trying to understand the way of defeating an opponent right from the moment he attacks. When the opponent attacks you, you should not block the attack, but step to the side and deflect the attacker forward. Because he continues forward along the attack line, he will be hit with double force by your Atemi to his eyes. After that he loses his balance and, thrown to the ground, he can be immobilized using different techniques.

Figure 1: Dori and Uke face each other in a left foot forward stance. As described earlier, Dori is completely relaxed.

Figure 2: Uke makes a large step with the right foot, intending to hit Dori on his left temple with Mawashi Uchi. In order to avoid the heavy punch, Dori has only got to make a half step back and outside to the left. Simultaneously he delivers a punch from below to the chin of the attacker. Even if the punch does not hit it is important to deliver it in this manner, because after extending the arm Dori draws it back and puts his palm near his left ear. Note that the movement of the forearm is not done from inside outwards but from below in a circular manner to Dori's own left ear.

Fighting stance Ai Hanmi – left foot leading

Half step back to the left side and Atemi with the left hand

3

While pulling the right foot to the left
Dori delivers a second Atemi to the eyes

4

Grasp Uke's right arm and pull it
towards you

5

While pulling the arm to the right,
Dori makes a large step behind Uke

6

Uke is thrown to the ground by a
turning motion

7

A mild technique for pinning Uke on
the ground

8

The alternative way to immobilize Uke
while free hands can be used to take
him out

Figure 3: Dori places his right foot to his left and draws his left hand back to his left ear, palm inside. Note that you should not lift your elbow up. Uke is pulled forward and will be hit by a devastating knuckle strike to his eyes called Shiraken Uchi.

Figure 4: After that strike, Dori grasps the wrist of the partner with his right hand still continuing to pull. Note that it is important to keep your elbow deep. For this reason Uke cannot use his left hand to counter by striking or pushing on the elbow.

Figure 5: Dori grasps Uke's right arm with both hands on the wrist and elbow and pulls it to the right side of his face while making a large step rearwards to the left.

Figure 6: Uke is thrown off balance and is taken to the ground by a sharp turn to the right with Tenkan Ashi. Simultaneously, Dori pulls on Uke's right arm and pushes the elbow to the ground. If done with full speed in a real fight, the opponent will crash very hard onto the ground and smash his face on the concrete.

Figures 7 and 8: In the Dojo, Dori leads Uke softly to the ground and pins him down by pushing his wrist onto the floor. Another method is to put the left knee onto the shoulder and the right one onto the palm. The advantage being that you can use both hands freely to manipulate Uke as you want.

PART VI
APPENDIX

List of the 15 described sword forms and the Aikido techniques:

Form	Name	Meaning	Chiburi	Aikido technique
1.	Shohatto Maegiri	Beginning of the sword-training by cutting forward	First	None
2.	Ukenagashi	Catching the attack and deflecting it	First	Ai Hanmi or Shomen Uchi No Ikkyo
3.	Ushirogiri	Cutting backwards	First	Kaiten Nage
4.	Zengogiri	Cutting forward and back	First	Ai Hanmi or Shomen Uchi No Shiho Nage
5.	Sayugiri	Cutting to the left and right	First	Gyaku Hanmi Shiho Nage
6.	Tsuka Osae	The attacker grasps the handle	First	Gyaku Hanmi Nikyo
7.	Tekubi Osae	The attacker grasps the wrist	First	Ai Hanmi Nikyo
8.	Kawashi Tsuki	Moving from one side to the other while stabbing	First	Jodan Tsuki No Sankyo

9.	Tsukekomi	Stick to the opponent and threaten him	Second	Jodan Tsuki No Kote Gaeshi
10.	Tsume	Put the opponent under continuous pressure	Second	Irimi Nage
11.	Sanpo	Cut in three directions	Second	Uchi Kaiten Sankyo
12.	Shiho	Cut in four directions	Third	Yokomen or Shomen Uchi No Shiho Nage
13.	Nukiawase	Draw the sword and line up to meet the attack	Fourth	Yokomen or Shomen Uchi No Gokyo
14.	Todome	Stop the attacker and 'kill' him immediately	First	Yonkyo
15.	Suemonogiri	Cutting something on a table	First	None

First Chiburl: style stems from Eishin Ryu
Second Chiburi: style stems from Katori Shinto Ryu
Third Chiburi: style stems from Suio Ryu
Fourth Chiburi: style stems from Suio Ryu

Terminology

Photo & Illustration Credits

Cover & Layout design:
Jens Vogelsang

Cover & Inside photos:
Thomas Martin,
Marco Meissner,
Kevin Russ,
Waldemar Thomanek pp. 2 and 12

Illustrations:
Michael Russ

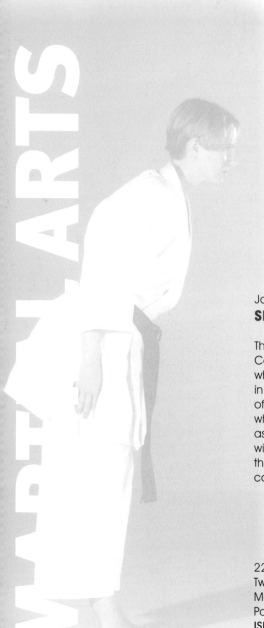

Shotokan Karate
KATA
Vol. 1

Joachim Grupp

Joachim Grupp
Shotokan Karate KATA Vol.1

The Kata are the backbone of Karate. Continually practising them allows the whole spectrum of possibilities contained in Karate to be revealed. The Kata consist of a fascinating multitude of techniques, which permit defence in close contact as well as at medium and long distance with your partner. Situations where the Kata can be applied are comprehensively explained in this book.

224 pages
Two-color print
More than 1,000 photos
Paperback, 5 $\frac{3}{4}$" x 8 $\frac{1}{4}$"
ISBN 1-84126-088-6
£ 12.95 UK/$ 17.95 US
$ 25.95 CDN/€ 16.90

MEYER
& MEYER
SPORT

MEYER & MEYER Sport | sales@windsorbooks.co.uk | www.m-m-sports.com

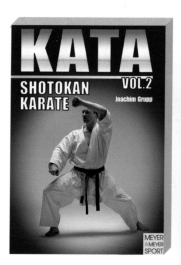

Joachim Grupp
Shotokan Karate KATA Vol.2

The Master Kata described in this book
belong to the advanced part of the
repertoire and carry on from the 17
basic and advanced Kata introduced
in Volume 1. This then completes the list
of all the Shotokan Karate Kata. There
are 9 Kata with Bunkai in this book:
Sochin, Meikyo, Chinte, Kanku-Sho,
Wankan, Ji'in, Jitte, Gankaku, Unsu.
There are more than 600 photos and
detailed descriptions, which allow a
deeper understanding of the Kata and
their application.

152 pages
Two-color print
682 photos
Paperback, $5^3/4$" x $8^1/4$"
ISBN 1-84126-091-6
£ 12.95 UK/$ 17.95 US
$ 25.95 CDN/€ 16.90

MEYER & MEYER Sport | sales@windsorbooks.co.uk | www.m-m-sports.com

MEYER
& MEYER
SPORT